SCIENCE & TECHNOLOGY IN FOCUS

SUPERCOMPUTERS

NEW EDITION

Charting the Future of Cybernetics

Charlene W. Billings and Sean M. Grady

Facts On File, Inc.

In loving memory of my parents
Alice Labbé Winterer
and
George Emil Winterer

SUPERCOMPUTERS: Charting the Future of Cybernetics, New Edition

Copyright © 2004 by Charlene W. Billings and Facts On File

This is a new edition of SUPERCOMPUTERS: *Shaping the Future*
by Charlene W. Billings (Facts On File, 1995)
Copyright © 1995 by Charlene W. Billings

Facts On File, Inc.
132 West 31st Street
New York NY 10001

Library of Congress Cataloging-in-Publication Data

Billings, Charlene W.
Supercomputers : Charting the future of cybernetics / Charlene W. Billings and Sean
M. Grady.— New Ed.
p. cm.
Includes bibliographical references.
ISBN 0-8160-4730-8
1. Supercomputers—Juvenile literature. I. Grady, Sean M., 1965– II.
Title
QA76.88.B54 2003
004.1′1—dc212003003628

Facts On File books are available at special discounts when purchased in bulk quantities for businesses, associations, institutions, or sales promotions. Please call our Special Sales Department in New York at (212) 967-8800 or (800) 322-8755.

You can find Facts On File on the World Wide Web at http://www.factsonfile.com

Text design by Erika K. Arroyo
Cover design by Nora Wertz
Illustrations by Sholto Ainslie

Printed in the United States of America

MP Hermitage 10 9 8 7 6 5 4 3 2 1

This book is printed on acid-free paper.

CONTENTS

ACKNOWLEDGMENTS

The authors wish to thank all those who provided information and photographs for this new edition of *Supercomputers*. In particular, they wish to thank Ellen Roder of Cray, Inc.; Dr. Lee A. Butler, U.S. Army Research Laboratory, Aberdeen Proving Ground; International Business Machines; the MITRE Corporation; Nobuo Shimakura of the Earth Simulator Center; Anne M. Stark and Julie Korhummel of the Lawrence Livermore National Laboratory; Dr. George A. Michael, formerly of the Lawrence Livermore National Laboratory, and Thomas M. DeBoni of the National Energy Research Scientific Computing Center; Hilary Kahn of the University of Manchester computer science department; Greg Lund and Gail Bamber of the San Diego Supercomputer Center; and Marvin G. Smith of NASA John H. Glenn Research Center at Lewis Field.

Special thanks also to Frank Darmstadt for patience and perseverance beyond the call of duty.

INTRODUCTION

Supercomputers are very fast, very powerful computers that can per-form trillions of mathematical operations in a second—sifting through geological survey data for oil companies that are seeking new deposits, analyzing readings taken during thunderstorms for meteorologists, simulating the forces of a nuclear explosion to test weapons designs and safety without conducting live tests.

Supercomputers also are the most cutting-edge, top-of-the-line computers on the market, and the most expensive ones—a status they have held since the early 1960s. Supercomputers are high-priced machines that require extra care and provide an advanced level of per-formance that most people do not need. Typical supercomputer cus-tomers are government and military agencies, academic institutions, and large corporations. Unlike the personal computers that are found in tens of millions of homes and offices, or the more advanced com-puters that form the backbone of the Internet, supercomputers have immense amounts of computational power and information storage capacity. Some supercomputer designs have had to include built-in refrigeration systems, while others have immersed their components in a bath of liquid coolant to keep them from overheating.

Though the term *supercomputer* was first used in the 1960s, com-puter companies such as IBM were building fast mainframe computers (large computers built with sturdy, often room-sized metal frames) as early as the mid-1950s. In a sense, all of the computers of this decade were supercomputers, with each new model designed to be faster and "smarter" than the ones before it. However, supercomputers in the modern sense did not exist until 1964, when the Control Data Corpo-ration brought the CDC 6600—an extremely fast computer designed by supercomputer pioneer Seymour Cray—to market. Its ability to perform 3 million floating-point operations (a type of calculation using decimal fractions) per second made it the fastest computer of its day—and a technological pipsqueak when compared to the supercomputers of today.

The path of development leading up to the supercomputer stretches back to the mid-17th century, when a French mathematician, Blaise Pascal, built a shoebox-sized mechanical counting machine that used cogs and gears to do calculations. Though the counter worked, it was too expensive to produce in great quantities and never became widely successful. Other inventors, though, designed and built various counting and calculating machines of their own over the next few hundred years. The most ambitious of these designs were the Difference Engine and the Analytical Engine, two mechanical, crank-operated computers designed in the mid-19th century by Charles Babbage, a British mathematician. Of the two designs, Babbage thought the analytical engine was the most promising. In his design, the analytical engine had the ability to store information, perform calculations, and retain the results for further operations, abilities that have been perfected in modern computers. Unfortunately, Babbage's plans were too advanced for the technology of Victorian England. Despite working nearly 20 years to translate his design from paper to reality, Babbage was unable to bring his creation to life. Nevertheless, because the functions of his mathematical engines were so close to those of modern computers, he is considered the founding father of computing.

During the 80 or so years following Babbage's attempt to build his complex calculator, other inventors invented or improved machines designed to make communicating easier and office chores less burdensome. Telephones, typewriters, cash registers, practical desktop calculators—these and other machines began appearing in homes and businesses around the world. But the most critical step toward the invention of computers in general, and supercomputers in particular, came in the last decade of the 19th century, when the U.S. Census Bureau used a punch card counting machine to analyze information gathered during the 1890 census. Working by hand, Census Bureau employees had taken 10 years to compile and tabulate the information gathered during the 1880 census; using the punch card counters, bureau employees working on the 1890 census took only two years.

From the time of the 1890 census to the middle of the 20th century, the development of computing technology gradually increased. Scientists in the United States and Europe who were studying the way information flowed through corporations and research institutions theorized that mechanical calculators could speed the process while reducing mistakes. Researchers for office machine companies also suggested building such machines to make doing business easier. And when World War II broke out in 1939, scientists in England began working on electronic code-cracking computers that could decipher the secret messages being relayed to the troops and ships of Nazi Germany.

These machines form the ancestry of supercomputers, which still are being used for many of the same tasks, such as cryptography and high-level accounting, that their predecessors were designed to handle. Just as with their home- and office-based counterparts, supercomputers have decreased in size and cost even as they have increased in computing power. Some computer industry analysts suggest that, with future advances, supercomputing power may be available for about as much money as a midrange personal computer cost in the late 1990s.

The two questions such predictions raise are "What would people use it for?" and "Are the advances needed for this type of supercomputer truly likely to happen?" Unless people use their computers for extremely complicated business or research tasks—such as creating detailed graphic displays or analyzing scientific data—much of the power of a supercomputer would be wasted in the average home or office. And as computer chip designers pack more components into tighter spaces, they are nearing the physical limits of how small electronics can go.

The answer to the first question likely will come from an unexpected source. Indeed, the personal computer, which came into being around 1975, did not catch on with consumers other than hobbyists and game players until almost 1980, when the first small-computer business spreadsheet program, VisiCalc, went into production. Likewise, the computer boom of the 1990s was sparked by the development of the World Wide Web and the Web browser in the late 1980s. These "killer applications," or "killer apps," took the world by surprise when they came out. The same thing may happen if a "killer app" for low-priced supercomputers comes along.

The second question, though, seems to be in the process of being solved. Optical computers that use light instead of electrons, computers that make use of quantum mechanics (a theory of how atoms and subatomic particles behave), and hypercomputers created from linking numerous computers into a computational network are being explored as methods to work around the physical limitations of computing.

Supercomputers: Charting the Future of Cybernetics is a revised and updated edition of *Supercomputers: Shaping the Future*, published in 1995 as part of Facts On File's Science Sourcebooks series. At that time, the field of supercomputing had nearly reached the point where these machines were able to perform 1 trillion floating-point operations per second, or "flops," per day. In fact, many of the companies that made these high-powered computers were building machines that theoretically could perform 2 or 3 trillion flops per second, though these systems did not reach this level of performance in real-world tests. At the end of 2001 the top 17 supercomputers in the world performed at or above the 1 trillion flop, or teraflop, calculation level— the most powerful, the IBM ASCI White computer at the Lawrence Livermore National Laboratory in California, performing nearly seven and a quarter teraflops when tested using a benchmarking program.

During this time, computer scientists and researchers also have figured out a number of ways to gain supercomputer-level performance from less expensive computing systems, including personal computers. These methods have been applied to such tasks as the search for new drugs to combat anthrax, a disease that long has been suggested as a possible weapon of bioterrorism, and which gained renewed attention because of a series of anthrax infections following the September 11, 2001, attacks on the World Trade Center in New York and the Pentagon in Washington, D.C.

This updated edition of *Supercomputers* gives students a good general idea of how the field of high-performance computing affects everyday life, not just the work of scientists and engineers. The following 19 chapters provide a closer look at how the supercomputers of today came to be, describe the makeup of typical supercomputer systems, provide examples of how supercomputers are used, and examine how the limits to future development are being confronted and overcome.

PART 1

Creating a
Calculating Machine

THE ORIGINAL COMPUTERS

Computers as we know them today are machines: boxes of circuit boards, wires, a few whirring fans, and a series of sockets for gadgets such as monitors and keyboards. This basic design is the same for just about every computer made today, from personal computers (PCs) to the most advanced supercomputers. Even Internet servers—which use fast central processing units (CPUs), large memory circuits, and gigabyte-capacity storage devices to send information from computer to computer over the world's phone lines—contain components that are not much different from those found in PCs.

These days, getting a computer to do more work means opening it up and putting in more memory cards, a more powerful CPU, or a larger hard-disk drive. Before the 1950s, though, getting more work from a computer meant providing better pay, better working conditions, and additional help from other computers. Yes, computers did exist back then; in fact, by the beginning of the 20th century, computers had existed for hundreds of years. They were not machines, however—they were people.

When it first became widely used (in about 1650), the word *computer* meant a person who performed mathematical computations for a living. Many of these human computers worked for banks, counting-houses (forerunners of modern-day accounting firms), trading companies, and other businesses that needed people who were good with numbers. Computers also worked for government agencies, universities, and scientific societies that wanted to prepare specialized numeric tables requiring complex mathematical work, such as almanacs showing the times of sunrise and sunset, or high and low tides.

It was not an ideal way to do business. All those calculations took a lot of time, and double-checking the human computers' output was a tedious process. Worse yet, there were no guarantees that the results of these efforts would be accurate (which, in many cases, they were not). Even though the work was done by men and women who were among the best-educated people of their times, there was a feeling throughout the world that there had to be a better way to do things. The search for this better way led to the creation of modern electronic computers, just as the desire to make basic arithmetic easier for the first human computers led to the development of mathematics.

Calculating by Hand

People who can handle numbers, from simple counting tasks to complex calculations, have been in demand just about as long as nations have existed. Some of the world's earliest writings—found on 5,200-year-old clay tablets from the ancient kingdom of Sumer, in what is now southern Iraq—are bookkeeping records that include tallies of crop yields and livestock produced in the land, of goods traded between cities, and of taxes taken in by the Sumerian kings and their governors. As people in other lands around the world began grouping together in towns, cities, and nations, they also began developing ways to keep track of these facts and figures. In a way, bookkeeping has been a major factor in the development of the world's written languages: The symbols people use today were developed over thousands of years by scribes who were, among other tasks, trying to keep up with the economics of their times.

As merchants expanded their trade to distant lands, their need for scribes who could keep track of this trade expanded as well. As kingdoms grew, their rulers needed people who could accurately keep track of the wealth in the royal treasuries and chart how it was spent on armies, palaces, and civic improvements such as sewers and city walls. Before long, the ability to manage information—collecting it, interpreting it, and sending it quickly to others—became a cornerstone of civilization.

Centuries passed, and people began to develop mathematical systems that went far beyond simple tasks of addition, subtraction, multiplication, and division. Elements of modern algebra, which focuses on general rules of arithmetic rather than operations with specific numbers, have been found in Egyptian scrolls dating back as far as 2,000 B.C. Modern algebra was developed by Greek, Hindu, and Arabic scholars; the word *algebra* comes from the Arabic word *al-jabr*, which means "the reunification."

Geometry—the system of measuring and calculating points, lines, angles, surfaces, and solid objects—probably got its start when ancient land surveyors discovered there were easily identified relationships between the proportions of objects. Scholars in many lands worked out a way to represent these relationships mathematically. This knowledge swiftly found its way into the building trades as architects and master craftsmen started to design mathematically based construction plans. The science of astronomy and the mysticism of astrology both were based on the mathematically predictable motion of the planets and the apparent motion of the Sun and the stars. Even art was seen as a realm in which mathematics played a part, with sculptors calculating ideal proportions for the objects they depicted and painters reproducing the appearance of the real world through use of vanishing points and other tricks of perspective.

Other methods that followed—trigonometry, logarithms, calculus, and further styles of advanced math—were developed by scholars who had the same goals as later computer pioneers: to make it easier to perform the mechanical operations of mathematics. To bring these mathematical systems into being, though, the scholars who created them needed a little help.

Beads, Sticks, and Wheels

People have always used some sort of tool to help them keep track of things. Before the scribes of Sumer came up with their accounting symbols, herders probably used piles of pebbles or notches in tree bark to keep track of how many cattle or sheep they had in their fields. We know this is possible, because modern-day herders across the globe do pretty much the same thing. Even the practice of mixing a few black sheep in a flock of white sheep is a method of keeping track of the flock, with a black sheep acting as a counter for 10 white ones.

Virtually anything could be used as a mathematical memory aid. The quipu, in which knotted strings were used to keep track of numbers such as population counts, was one of the more unusual of these devices.

Developed by the Inca civilization in what is now the South American nation of Peru, the quipu was a cord with long strings of different colors tied along its length. The Incas recorded numbers by tying patterns of knots along the string, starting at the bottom with the units and moving up for tens, hundreds, thousands, and so on. The number 4 was indicated with a group of four knots tied close together at the bottom of the string; 34 was a group of four knots at the bottom of the string and a group of three knots above it, with a small space to show the jump from units to tens; 234 was, from bottom to top, a group of four knots, a space, a group of three knots, a space, and then two knots. Recording larger numbers simply meant tying more groups of knots. When the cord was mounted or held horizontally, someone who was trained in the art of knot recording easily could read it.

Other cultures came up with different mechanisms, ones that helped their users calculate as well as count. Counting boards were particularly widespread; these were wooden planks or slabs of wood with lines or spaces inscribed upon their surface. Using stone, metal, or wood counters, people could tally objects and perform simple arithmetic, with the counters serving as reminders of where their work was going. Historians believe counting boards were designed to mimic a system that involved moving pebbles along lines drawn in sand or dirt, with each line representing progressively higher values (a line for ones, a line for tens, a line for hundreds).

A popular method in ancient China was the use of rod numerals—symbols of horizontal and vertical lines that represented numbers—and rod counters made of ivory, metal, or other materials that could be used to recreate rod numerals on counting boards. By moving the rod counters to recreate the shapes of the rod numerals, people could calculate sums and differences.

Eventually, an even better device came along that largely replaced rod counters in Asia, though counting boards still were used there and in the Western world. The abacus—which seems to have been developed independently near the eastern coast of the Mediterranean Sea and in Asia—is a series of sliding beads mounted in rows on a horizontal or vertical framework. As with the counters on a counting board, the beads can be used both to count objects and to perform basic arithmetic—addition, subtraction, multiplication, and division—by shifting them in certain patterns. Multiplication and division were harder than addition and subtraction, especially when large numbers were involved, but experienced abacus users were able to perform these tasks easily.

ABACUS

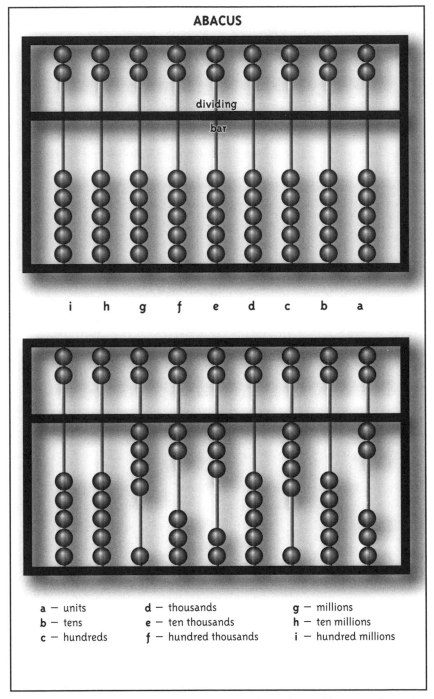

dividing bar

i h g f e d c b a

a — units		**d** — thousands		**g** — millions	
b — tens		**e** — ten thousands		**h** — ten millions	
c — hundreds		**f** — hundred thousands		**i** — hundred millions	

Rapid and accurate, the abacus was used throughout the world as a mathematical tool. Even today, many people living in Asian nations prefer it to electronic calculators. The bottom abacus is set to show the total 4,230,402.

The drawback to all this shifting around, of course, was that the abacus could not be used to store numbers; one sharp bump, and the record would be scrambled. Keeping track of results meant writing them down. Even so, for the better part of 2,000 years, scientists, book-keepers, and government officials throughout the world used abacuses and counting boards to perform most of their calculations. With only a few other tools available, mathematicians and philosophers created or wrote down the foundations for advanced forms of mathematics such as algebra, trigonometry, and solid geometry, as well as tasks such as the calculation of square and cube roots and calculations involving fractions.

In fact, the use of the abacus was the reason that the Romans never developed a substitute for their unwieldy numerals, with I representing ones, V fives, X tens, C hundreds, and so on. Decoding the Roman numeral MCMLXII means working through the following analysis:

"M" means 1,000. "C" means 100, unless it comes before an "M," in which case it means "take 100 away from 1,000," leaving 900. "L" means 50, "X" means 10, and "I" means 1; add their values together to get 62. Therefore, "MCMLXII" is 1,000 plus 900 plus 62, or 1,962.

This method rendered simple amounts such as 347 as CCCXXXXVII (three hundreds, four tens, a five, and two ones). Using an abacus to perform their calculations meant that all the Romans had to do was shift beads and write down the results—a much easier way of doing things than, for example, trying to add MCMLXII and CCCXXXXVII by hand on paper.

The numbers most of the world uses today came from India and the Muslim world—though very slowly, first appearing in Europe in the eighth century A.D. and not becoming the standard means of writing numerical values until the 17th century. Hindu and Arabic scholars sought a way to make the symbols themselves do the work of the counting boards and abacuses. The advantage to the Hindu-Arabic numbers was that there were only 10 of them—the symbols 1 through 9 and the place-holding symbol, 0—yet they could be used to write any value with little need for interpretation. The numeric symbols and the way they are written today, with each decimal value in a fixed place and the symbol 0 as a placeholder, made it easier to handle numbers.

Even so, mathematicians constantly sought to make their work even more rapid. In the early 17th century, mathematician and Scottish baron John Napier came up with a way to avoid the problems of mul-tiplying and dividing on an abacus by using a new method of calcula-tion that he invented. In effect he sliced up the multiplication table in

"Napier's Bones" was the nickname given to this mechanical calculator, which Scottish mathematician John Napier devised as a faster way to perform multiplication and division. [© Public Record Office/Topham-HIP/The Image Works]

such a way that it could be recorded on a series of rectangular rods that were fitted onto a wooden frame. Depending on the pattern, and with enough rods, the user could multiply or divide any two whole numbers.

The rods, or "Napier's Bones" as they were called, became popular throughout Europe in the decades following their invention. Some models used cylindrical rods mounted side by side in boxes, with knobs that were used to spin the rods into the correct configuration. Other mathematicians built their own calculating gizmos, some of which were based on Napier's Bones. One of these early calculators used not only a version of the bones, but mechanical gears that automatically performed basic addition and subtraction. Called the "calculating clock," it was built by a German scholar named Wilhelm Schickard in 1623. Unfortunately, war interrupted Schickard's work on the machine, and Schickard died of bubonic plague in 1635. We know of the calculating clock today because of a few drawings that survived the scholar's death, which allowed a working version of the machine to be built in 1960.

The route to the calculators and computers of today got its start with another 17th-century scholar: Blaise Pascal, the son of a French lawyer and tax commissioner who was an acknowledged mathematical genius by the time he was 16 years old. In the 1680s, while he was in his early 20s, Pascal designed a working adding machine to help make his father's work as a tax collector a bit easier. Pascal and his father often worked late into the night calculating the taxes owed to and collected by the government using counting boards, and both wished for a faster way to get the job done.

Though Pascal did not know of Schickard's calculating clock, his adding machine also used hand-operated gears to perform the addition and subtraction needed for tax work. Called the Pascaline, the shoe-box-sized calculator had a row of up to eight numbered dials on top for entering numbers. An equal number of small numbered cylinders displayed the answers, which could be read though small holes in the Pascaline's lid. Connecting the dials to the cylinders was a complex arrangement of gears and ratchets that performed the calculation of the sums and differences.

The Pascaline earned its inventor even more fame among scholars and royalty than he had before, as much for showing that a machine could perform mathematical tasks as for building the machine itself. Despite this fame, though, the Pascaline did not come into general use for a couple of reasons. First, the mechanism had an unfortunate tendency to slip its gearing and generate errors, which made people wonder about its reliability. And although it could add and subtract, it could not do anything else. Combined with the fact that each Pascaline cost about as much as most well-off French citizens spent in a year (each calculator was handmade and pushed the limits of 17th-century French craftsmanship) the machine's drawbacks discouraged all but a few people from bringing one into home or office.

However, Pascal's invention encouraged the invention of other calculators—most of which failed to work and generally were forgotten. The one great exception was a calculator called the "stepped reckoner," which was invented by another famous 17th-century scholar, Gottfried Wilhelm von Leibniz, whose greatest claim to fame was the creation of a form of the mathematical system of calculus that became world's standard.

Like the Pascaline, the stepped reckoner was designed to use a series of gears to calculate sums and differences, as well as to do most of the work involved in multiplication and division. The machine was not fully automatic. It was covered with dials, knobs, pegs, and cranks that had to be adjusted before and during each operation. What made it revolutionary was the Leibniz wheel, a cylinder-shaped gear Leibniz designed with nine teeth that ran only partway down the side of the cylinder. The first tooth was one-tenth the length of the gear, the second was two-tenths the length, the third was three-tenths the length, all the way to the last tooth, which was nine-tenths the length. When connected to the other gears and mechanisms, the Leibniz wheels performed the musclework of the stepped reckoner's calculations.

Or at least they would have, if the machine had worked reliably. Unfortunately, the stepped reckoner, like the Pascaline, was too complex a mechanism for its time. Leibniz worked on a demonstration model of the machine for more than 20 years but was never able to get it to work.

Tide Tables and Insurance Charts

By the 19th century, the limitations of human computing were beginning to create problems. The great voyages of discovery, the founding of new nations and expansion of empires, and the ever-increasing trade in and between the countries of the world had created ever-increasing amounts of paperwork. Progress meant dealing with shipping records, taxes, population counts, bank accounts, loan rates, insurance company statistics, and a world of other information, all of which had to be calculated and organized by hand.

Great Britain's *Nautical Almanac*, a book of navigational tables (times of high and low tides throughout the world, sunrise and sunset times at different latitudes, and similar information), was an example of this work in action. Produced every year, starting in 1766, by the Royal Observatory, the almanac was the first such volume in history to be published as the result of an ongoing, large-scale tabulation project. Until then, information tables were produced either by small staffs of full-time mathematicians hired by governments, universities, scientific societies, and merchants' associations who needed frequent updates, or by large groups assembled for one-time jobs, such as preparing tables of geometric functions for land surveyors.

At first, the almanac owed its existence to the work of freelance "computers," who lived throughout Britain. Mostly clergymen or clerks who wanted to work after their retirement, these calculators worked in teams of three: two who calculated and a third who double-checked the work. The computers were hired based on their reliability with mathematical tasks, and they worked at home where they could concentrate on the often-complex calculations. Britain's royal astronomer, together with his staff, supervised the work.

Despite the close attention paid to the work, significant errors often found their way into the final version of each year's *Nautical Almanac*, especially during a 20-year period in the early 19th century when the book became notorious for providing faulty information. Even small errors could create havoc for ships around the world. More than once, a captain found his vessel scraping the bottom of a harbor channel, or even running aground on a sandbar, because a table that showed the time that a high tide would come in was off by a few minutes, leading him to sail across an area where there was too little water beneath his ship.

The business world also suffered when it used inaccurate math tables. In particular, the insurance industry of the 19th century, which saw a big expansion thanks to the Industrial Revolution, needed correct actuarial tables. Actuarial tables contain statistical information that insurers use when they decide whether to issue an insurance policy. An actuarial table can show the average life expectancy of men and women in a given nation, the chance that a building will burn down in a particular city during a decade, or the probability that a ship will be sunk by a hurricane before it delivers a cargo. Because so many factors play a part in calculating these tables—weather, health, accidents, even simple bad luck—it is not hard to make a small error that can end up costing a company thousands of dollars.

Fortunately, the 19th century also was a time of great innovation and invention. During that time, three things happened that not only led to a greater accuracy in the way information was handled but also led directly to the creation of modern computers.

2

ANALYTICAL ENGINES AND CENSUS WEAVERS

The path that led to the creation of computers, and from there to supercomputers, was turning out to be a trail of false starts, of alternating successes and failures. Though Wilhelm Schickard was able to build a working model of his "calculating clock," its accidental destruction and Schickard's death kept it from having any influence on later designs. On the other hand, Blaise Pascal and Gottfried Leibniz had trouble getting their calculators to work, but their ideas became famous and inspired other inventors.

From 1620 to the middle of the 19th century, many scholars used the cylindrical gears Leibniz invented, along with components of their own, in their attempts to mechanize mathematics. Most of these devices worked poorly, if at all. The few that did work were seen as clever examples of craftsmanship, but they were not considered practical substitutes for human brainpower. They tended to malfunction, and, like the Pascaline and the stepped reckoner, they were expensive to build. It made more sense to continue paying people to calculate.

Things started changing in the early 1800s. By then, the Industrial Revolution, which started when Scottish engineer James Watt patented an improved steam engine, was beginning to remake the

13

Western world. The development of highly advanced machine tools and the construction of the first modern factories convinced people that machines could be trusted to perform complicated tasks. These machines made it possible for craftsmen to turn out intricate mechanisms that worked reliably. One of these devices was a calculator that truly worked, which Thomas de Colmar, a French industrialist who was the director of an insurance company, built in 1820.

Called the Arithmometer, the calculator used Leibniz wheels to calculate the tables of figures that de Colmar's company needed. The device was sturdy, reliable, and accurate, churning out long lists of figures as its users turned a crank on the front of its cabinet. The Arithmometer had its limitations, of course: setting it up for a series of calculations took a long time, which meant that using it took about as much time as an average human clerk took to do the same work. On the other hand, the machine made up for its slow speed with its reliability and accuracy.

There was one other difference between the Arithmometer and all the other calculators: it was a commercial success. Enough people across Europe were eager to buy one of the machines for their businesses or for use in research—and had the money to afford one of these high-tech gadgets—to encourage de Colmar to open a small calculator factory. Within a couple of decades, de Colmar's calculator was competing with similar products made by other companies, and the office machine industry was born. This development was good for businesses and other institutions with routine math needs. But what about the people who needed to do more complex calculations, such as those for navigation tables and so forth?

An English mathematician named Charles Babbage thought he knew how to make those tasks easier as well, and he spent his life trying to do so.

Charles Babbage's Mathematical "Engines"

About the time that de Colmar was building his first Arithmometer, Babbage and an astronomer named John Herschel were double-checking a list of figures for the Royal Astronomical Society of Great Britain. As with any other set of calculations, the one Babbage and Herschel were working on was riddled with errors. After a few hours

Though his calculating "engines" never reached the working stage, British mathematician Charles Babbage is considered the intellectual ancestor of the modern computer. (Courtesy IBM Archives)

labor, Babbage said he wished the list "had been executed by steam." The idea of a reliable steam-powered calculator appealed to Herschel as well. He and Babbage briefly discussed ways that such a machine could be built; Babbage continued thinking about the problem until he came up with a way to make it work.

Babbage's idea was for a machine that churned out lists of numbers by using a method called the sum of differences. The method is based on a simple math trick: Think of a set of numbers, such as the odd numbers: 1, 3, 5, 7, 9, and so on. The difference between one number and the next, the value left when the smaller is subtracted from the larger, is always 2. That means the next number in the series can be found simply by adding 2 to the previous number: 9+2=11, 11+2=13.

The same trick can be performed on many sets of numbers as long as there is a constant progression from one number to the next—as long as the sequence of numbers is not created at random. By subtracting adjacent numbers in the set, and then repeatedly subtracting adjacent numbers in the sets generated from the first one, it is possible to reach a point where the difference value is a constant number. Then the process can be reversed to find the next number in the original set. Computers—the human kind, of course—often used the difference method to calculate and check mathematical tables because it was a quick and easy way to get the job done. Still, where a human might make a mistake in addition, a machine would not, Babbage decided.

He designed a machine to make use of this method of differences. It would be a two-ton collection of steam-powered gears, rods, and ratchet arms in a frame measuring 10 feet high, 10 feet wide, and five feet thick. The starting values for each calculation would be dialed in by hand, and the type of list generated would be determined by changing the starting position of the gears. There even would be a kind of printer attached to it, one that would stamp the results of the machine's work on metal printing plates that could be used to make paper copies of the tables. Babbage named his creation the Difference Engine.

The Difference Engine, its designer knew, would be one of the most complex mechanisms ever built. He also knew that he would need to hire skilled machinists to put the engine together, and he knew that building it would require more money than he had. He solved both problems by convincing the British government to help pay for the device, knowing that the nation was desperate for some way to improve the accuracy of its *Nautical Almanac* and other tables. By fall 1823, Babbage had received the equivalent of roughly $121,000 from the government (which would end up spending the equivalent of $1.3 million more on the project), had converted three rooms of his house into a workshop, and had hired a mechanical engineer, Joseph Clement, to serve as the Difference Engine's chief engineer.

This period pretty much marked the high point of the project. As happened to many other inventors, Babbage had designed a machine that was too advanced for the technology of his time. The gears were oddly shaped and were difficult to shape using the tools of the time. The engine's parts had to fit together so tightly that any dirt in the machine, and even the expansion of the gears from the heat generated as the machine operated, could have thrown off the engine's operation. However, the mathematician was too stubborn to change his design; he refused to take shortcuts or alter the Difference Engine so it could be built with available tools. Instead, he and Clement spent much of the project's early years developing tools that could be used to make the machine.

Technology was not the only hurdle. As chief engineer, Clement ran the machine shop where the engine was being built, and he made up the list of expenses for his part of the operation. Babbage constantly fought with Clement over costs: Babbage suspected that Clement was exaggerating his claims simply to make more money, but there was no proof. Together, Clement's high operating costs and Babbage's perfectionism slowed work dramatically. Even so, by 1832 Babbage and Clement were able to build a small portion of the Difference Engine, which they successfully demonstrated to a group of government officials.

Assembling that section of the machine turned out to be the end of the Difference Engine. Soon after the demonstration, Babbage and Clement had a final battle over the budget. Babbage refused to agree to Clement's latest demands for payment, and Clement went on strike for a year. He fired his workers, closed his shop, and locked up the plans for the engine. Without proof that Clement was lying about his expenses, there was nothing Babbage could do. The law was on Clement's side—he even was allowed to keep the machine tools that had been built with the government's money, thanks to a law saying tools belonged to the workman who used them.

Eventually, Babbage and the government gave in. Clement got his money, Babbage got the plans back, and the government wrote off the project as a loss. By that time, though, Babbage had lost interest in the Difference Engine. He had thought of a new and better machine.

Programmable Looms

Babbage called his new creation the Analytical Engine. It was analytical because, unlike the Difference Engine, it would be able to analyze and act on a set of instructions fed into it. Where the Difference Engine would have been restricted to one form of calculating, the Analytical Engine would handle nearly any mathematical task.

Instructions for this new engine would be encoded on punch cards, cardboard rectangles covered with patterns of holes that could be read by spring-loaded pins that either passed through the holes or were blocked by the card. One set of punch cards would prepare the machine to calculate, another set would provide the numbers the machine was to use, and a third set would contain math tables and other extra information the machine would need for its work.

The idea to use punch cards came from the French weaving industry. In the 1720s a weaver named Basile Bouchon built a loom that was controlled by a pattern of holes punched in long strips of paper. Pins pressed down on the strip to "read" the instructions; levers connected to the pins controlled most of the loom's actions, though the loom needed a human operator to manage some of its functions. Other weavers improved on the design until 1804, when Joseph-Marie Jacquard built a loom that was fully automatic, powered by a small steam engine, and able to weave a bolt of cloth, a tapestry, or any other fabric by itself. Instead of punched tape, it used a strip of punch cards that were sewn together to make a belt of instructions. To demonstrate the loom's abilities, Jacquard set it up to weave detailed black-and-white portraits of himself, a job that required 10,000 punch cards to hold all the instructions. Babbage had one of these pieces of fabric art, which inspired him to adapt the punch card system for his calculator.

The Analytical Engine was a far more complicated machine than Jacquard's loom or the Difference Engine. Its design eventually covered nearly 7,000 pages of notes and 1,000 pages of drawings and

A few sets of the analytical engine's computational wheels survived as museum pieces, thanks to Charles Babbage's son, Henry. [Courtesy IBM Archives]

designs for its towers of gears, wheels, and rods. One row of gear towers kept hold of the numbers entered into the machine. Babbage called this area the "store"—today it would be called the Analytical Engine's memory. A larger collection of gears formed the "mill," where the calculations took place. There even was a control unit that made sure the mill started working only after all the starting values had been pulled out of the store, and that the results were saved or printed out before the engine started its next set of calculations.

With the Analytical Engine, Babbage had invented a machine with nearly every major component of a modern-day computer. In addition to mechanical versions of a central processing unit (made up of the mill and the control unit) and a memory, it had input devices (the punchcard readers), an output device (a typesetting machine like the Difference Engine's), and a form of long-term data storage, the punch cards. Unlike true computers, though, it could not permanently store programs for later use, but had to be reprogrammed each time a new operation was needed. Instead, the Analytical Engine was a locomotive-sized programmable calculator.

At least it would have been, if it had been built. When Babbage tried to find the money to build his new calculator, he discovered that no one wanted to get involved with it. The British government, which decided that one failed Babbage project was enough, was particularly uninterested in the mathematician's new design. Babbage's perfectionism also sabotaged the construction of the Analytical Engine—the calculator's designer could not stop designing the calculator. Each time he finished the plans for one section of the machine, he thought of a better way to redesign another.

Babbage had just enough money to support his obsession for the rest of his life. As with the Difference Engine, though, only a small section of the Analytical Engine was ever built. It calculated and printed a table of multiples of pi (the ratio between a circle's circumference and its diameter). Unfortunately, Babbage never saw this small victory. He died in 1871, and Henry Babbage, his son, built the device in the mid-1880s as part of a failed attempt to complete his father's work.

Having come very close to achieving his goals, and to having nearly invented a computer in the middle of the 19th century, Charles Babbage ended as a discouraged and somewhat scorned figure. Even so, it would be a mistake to think of his work on the two engines as a complete failure. Other mathematicians, engineers, and inventors around the world read about Babbage's work on the Difference Engine and designed difference calculators of their own. Some of these machines were used for scientific and statistical work. A Swedish calculator called the Tabulating Machine won a gold medal at a world exhibition in Paris in 1855, with a good deal of support from Babbage. A few years later, an American observatory bought it and used it to help calculate the orbit of Mars.

(In a sad twist of fate, Britain's Register General, the government agency that kept records of birth rates, death rates, and other statistics, paid for a version of the Tabulating Machine that was used to calculate more than 600 tables for the insurance industry and for other purposes.)

Pins, Quicksilver, and the 1890 Census

Even the Analytical Engine can be seen as a signpost on the path to computers. Babbage had been on the right track when he decided to use the Jacquard loom's punch cards to program the machine. Punch cards were a compact and accurate way of recording data, and they would be used in a real calculating machine built to pull the United States away from the threshold of a political crisis.

According to the U.S. Constitution, there has to be a physical count of every person living in the nation once every decade. An accurate count of citizens, called a census, is a vital part of figuring how many people each state sends to Congress. The U.S. Senate is made up of two senators from each state. However, the House of Representatives is divided among the states based on their populations: The states with the bigger populations get more seats in the House. When the Census Bureau started its work in 1790, counting heads and adding up the total by hand was an easy matter—considering there were only about 4 million people in the 15 states that made up the nation at that time. As the country and its population grew, the work took longer to complete, and the final count came out later and later.

Things got really bad during the census of 1880. Counting every man, woman, and child in the United States, which took less than a year, was the easy part. Adding up the numbers—which included statistics on each citizen's age, sex, occupation, level of literacy, and other factors—took years. As early as 1881 the U.S. Census Bureau realized that the results would not be ready until nearly the end of the decade and would be badly out of date. The bureau also realized that by the beginning of the 20th century, the results of one decade's census would not be ready until after the next decade's census had started.

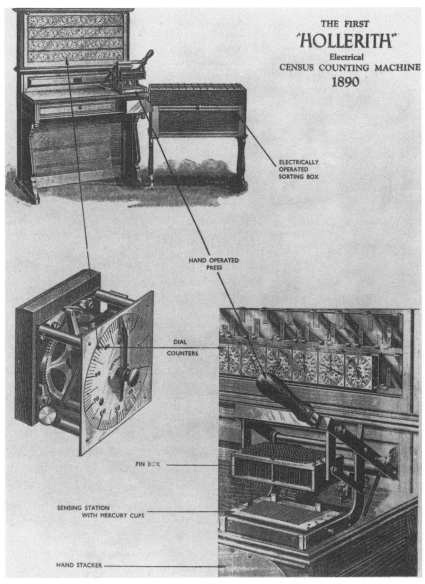

THE FIRST
"HOLLERITH"
Electrical
CENSUS COUNTING MACHINE
1890

ELECTRICALLY
OPERATED
SORTING BOX

HAND OPERATED
PRESS

DIAL
COUNTERS

PIN BOX

SENSING STATION
WITH MERCURY CUPS

HAND STACKER

Created by Herman Hollerith, the census tabulator used punch cards to store data and was a mechanical precursor of the modern computer. [Courtesy IBM Archives]

The nation never reached that point, thanks to a Census Bureau agent and mechanical engineer named Herman Hollerith. Late in the summer of 1881, Hollerith and his supervisor were discussing the problem of the 1880 count. Hollerith later wrote that his supervisor gave him the idea "of a machine for doing the purely mechanical work of tabulating population and similar statistics . . . using cards with the description of the individual shown by notches punched on the edge of the card."

Hollerith pursued his supervisor's idea, though at first he tried using a wide paper punch tape to record each citizen's information, rather than the notched cards his supervisor had mentioned. Why did he choose punch tape? No one knows for sure, but it may have struck him as a better method of recording data for the first machine he designed. When the tape ran through the machine, it passed between a metal drum and a series of thin metal wires. Wherever there was a hole in the paper tape, a wire would come in contact with the drum, and a small electric current would flow up the brush to a circuit that registered the signal on a counter.

The device worked, but Hollerith soon realized that a punch card system would be better for the task. Punch tape had one serious drawback: Because it contained all its information on a single long strip, there was no easy way to find a single record or a series of records. The entire tape would have to run through the machine, and a clerk would have to keep an eye out for the information he or she needed. Hollerith redesigned his system to use punch cards on which the information was punched not around the edges but in boxes within the cards. Each hole in a punch card represented one of the facts about an individual that the government wanted to know.

A small, hand-operated press served as the card reader. Hundreds of metal pins were attached to the top of the press; a matching bed of small cups filled with mercury, a metal that is liquid at room temperature, was on the bottom. The press was mounted on a desk beneath a panel of electric dial counters, and an electrically operated sorting box was connected to the desk with a wire cable. As each card was processed, some pins would pass through the holes in the card and dip into the mercury, completing an electric circuit. The dials on top of the desk were wired into those circuits; as a card was read, the appropriate dials would advance one position and the lid on one of the slots in the sorting box would pop open. All the clerk who was running the cards through the machine had to do was insert the card in the reader, press down the reader's handle, and put the card in the open slot.

When Hollerith presented his tabulation machine to the Census Bureau toward the end of the 1880s, the bureau tested it against two advanced hand-counting methods it was considering for use in the 1890 count. The test used census forms for 10,491 people living in St. Louis, Missouri. It took more than 72 hours to punch the raw data onto the cards, but once that task was completed, the machine tabulated the information in less than six hours. Clerks using the fastest hand-counting method took more than 155 hours to finish the entire job.

The Census Bureau ordered 56 tabulators to be delivered to Washington, D.C., where they went into action in July 1890. Using the machines, the clerks of the Census Bureau were able to complete their work on the 1890 census in a little less than seven years. Thanks to another special-purpose counting machine Hollerith invented, the clerks were able to come up with a total figure for the U.S. population—62,622,250—a mere six weeks after they started their work.

News of the remarkable success of Hollerith's tabulation machines spread across the world, and Hollerith—who had started a business, the Tabulating Machine Company, to capitalize on his invention—soon began receiving orders. Foreign governments needed the tabulators for their own census work, and large companies realized they could adapt the machines to provide much-needed assistance in their inventory and accounting departments. Soon, the Tabulating Machine Company, which leased its machines rather than selling them so it could have a guaranteed steady stream of income, had more orders than it could fill.

More important, the success of the tabulator drew attention to the speed and accuracy that machines could achieve. Before long, people would find ways to harness this power in ways the inventors of the past never could have imagined.

3

AUTOMATING THE OFFICE

Herman Hollerith's counting machine was a direct ancestor of today's computers and supercomputers. It was one of the first successful machines to process information electrically, which is the main task of today's computers. It stored information in an easy-to-manage, easy-to-use form. And it used a mechanism, its punch card reader, that went on to become a standard data-entry device in the first few decades of the computer age.

The tabulator also helped create the industry that would in turn advance the development of computers. Before the mid-1880s most big business had no use for mechanical devices. Even though the Arithmometer and competing calculators found their way into insurance companies, engineering firms, and some universities, they were too slow for ordinary accounting tasks. A well-trained bookkeeper could add a column of numbers in far less time than it took to set up the machines and crank them through their computations.

Things changed after 1885, when a handful of inventors developed new calculators—as well as typewriters, cash registers, and other office appliances—that worked well enough to speed up the way businesses operated. News of the Hollerith tabulator's performance during the 1890 census helped spur the use of these machines around the world. From 1895 to the mid-1930s the business world served as a research and development laboratory for this new technology. Each company that adopted the new machines became an experiment in the application of office automation; success was shown in lower expenses and higher profits.

Typewriters and Number Crunchers

The clacking of manual typewriters and the crunching of mechanical desktop calculators at work have all but disappeared from the background noise of modern offices. Desktop computers, with their quietly clicking keyboards, and silent digital calculators have taken over most of the workload from these machines. At the beginning of the 20th century, though, the impact of type bars on paper and the grinding of number wheels within an adding machine were the sounds of progress.

The devices that mechanized the business world were strictly mechanical—even when powered by electricity, they used gears, levers, counting wheels, and other bits of machined metal to do their work. Early models were clumsy to use and needed frequent repairs—a common problem with any new technology. The first businesses that used them gained an immediate advantage over their competitors, however. Before long, no business could function successfully without at least one of these devices.

Office work around the time that Hollerith began developing his tabulator shows why office automation was such a crucial factor in the development of modern computers and supercomputers. With few exceptions, 19th-century offices were run by penmanship. Every business document, whether a simple receipt from a general store or a business letter between two company presidents, was written by hand. If a large company wanted a record of its letters, shipping receipts, or other paperwork, it hired a staff of clerks who copied the documents word by word into blank books before the originals left the building.

All this writing and copying took a lot of time, and deciphering less-readable documents was one of the hurdles that company executives had to face each day. For a business to run smoothly, its copyists needed to write at least 25 words per minute; any slower, and important letters or orders might not be sent out in time. Secretaries had to have the same level of writing skills, and a manager's success in a company sometimes was the result of his having readable handwriting.

Starting around 1850, a number of inventors tried to develop a mechanical solution to these problems, but none of their devices worked. These early typewriters either were too difficult to operate—one design had its letter and number keys on a disk that was dialed by hand—or were far too slow to replace even an average copy clerk. Then a former newspaper editor, Christopher Shoales, figured out a way to solve the speed problem.

Shoales used a keyboard, rather than dials or pointers, as the input device for his typewriter. Each key was connected to a bar of type that swung up and stamped a letter or number on the page. These type bars were arranged in a semicircular "basket" pattern that took up the least amount of space and allowed typists to see what they were working on. Shoales's first typewriters only had capital letters, and their type bars often collided and locked together. The design worked well enough, however, for Shoals to convince someone to provide financial backing for the improvements his typewriter needed.

In solving the collision problem, Shoales created a standard for office machines that would last for more than a century. The type bars had collided because the first keyboard design allowed people to type faster than the type bars could move. Shoales redesigned the keyboard to make these letters less easy to find, forcing typists to slow down to a speed the machine could handle. The new keyboard had Q,W,E,R,T, and Y in the topmost row of letters; thus, the design became known as the QWERTY pattern. Other typewriter manufacturers adopted this pattern as well, and it became so widely used that even today's computer keyboards still use the 19th-century arrangement.

The ability to type lowercase as well as capital letters came later, after Shoales's financial backer found a manufacturer capable of assembling the typewriter at a reasonable cost. E. Remington and Sons, a New York gun maker that had been looking for other ways to make money, produced 1,000 typewriters in 1874. These first models sold slowly, as few potential customers knew that a working typewriter had been produced and fewer still were willing to try out the new machines. By 1880, though, a revised typewriter was on the market—the Remington Model 2, which had a shift key that allowed people to write using uppercase and lowercase letters—and the company was selling 1,000 machines a year. By 1900, more than 10 other companies were competing with Remington, and they were shipping more than 100,000 typewriters out of their factories each year.

Mechanical calculators were beginning to achieve similar levels of sales at the turn of the 20th century. The Arithmometer and other machines based on its design were complicated. Users had to turn knobs, adjust dials, and spin cranks in order to get the figures they needed. After doing all this work, the users had to write down the answers, as the machines did not have printers.

Convenience came to calculators in the 1880s, thanks to two American inventors. The first of these, Dorr E. Felt, was a 24-year-old Chicago machinist whose design echoed an innovation of the Shoales typewriter: It had a keyboard. Felt's Comptometer had up to 10 columns of keys that were numbered from 1 to 9, with a row of dials at the bottom of the keyboard that showed the numbers as they were entered. Springs and levers connected the keys to the mechanism that spun the dials. Though the machine could only add and subtract, it did these tasks very well. In 1887, Felt and Robert Tarrant, a Chicago-area manufacturer, began making the Comptometer for sale to banks and other businesses. Two years later, Felt designed a new model that printed a record of the numbers entered and their totals on a strip of paper.

As successful as Felt and Tarrant became—their company was selling more than 1,000 machines a year at the beginning of the 20th century—they enjoyed only a brief monopoly. Another inventor, William S. Burroughs, created a printing calculator in 1892, following his creation of a hand-cranked device that proved to be too fragile for everyday business use when it went to market in 1887. Burroughs's machine soon became the industry leader, though the Comptometer sold well until the 1950s.

Efficiency Experts and Office Automation

Swift though they were when compared to unaided human labor, the typewriter and the adding machine faced an obstacle that was almost unbeatable—tradition. Businesses used their awkward records systems, slow billing practices, and other nonmechanical methods because these techniques had proven reliable over time. In many nations, the financial institutions of banking, insurance, accounting, and stock trading had developed a way of doing business that made it all but impossible for them to adopt the new technology that was developing in America. The effort and expense of abandoning these decades-old, and sometimes centuries-old, practices simply would cost too much and be too much of a business disruption.

Even in the United States, where traditional business methods were not as deeply entrenched as they were in Europe, people were reluc-

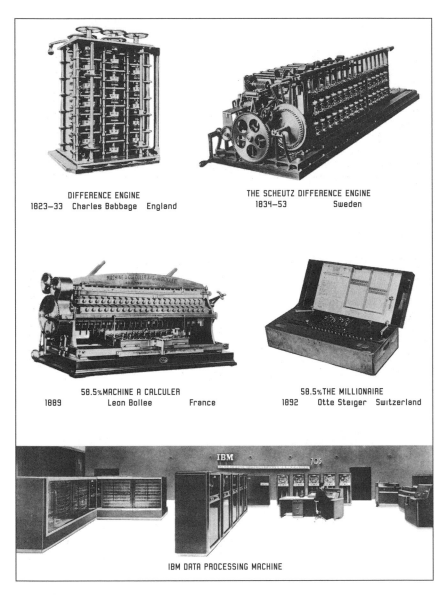

DIFFERENCE ENGINE
1823–33 Charles Babbage England

THE SCHEUTZ DIFFERENCE ENGINE
1834–53   Sweden

58.5%MACHINE A CALCULER
1889   Leon Bollee   France

58.5%THE MILLIONAIRE
1892   Otte Steiger Switzerland

IBM DATA PROCESSING MACHINE

During the 1950s, IBM traced the concept of mechanical calculators and data processing back to Babbage's difference engine. [Courtesy IBM Archives]

tant to change. They needed to be convinced that the expense and trouble of installing new machines would result in a more efficient operation and, thus, bigger profits. Often, they needed to be shown that their current methods were slowing them down, putting them at risk of being driven out of business by well-organized competitors.

Here is where the efficiency expert came in. Also called systematizers, efficiency experts were similar to modern-day business consultants: They analyzed how companies worked and showed them how they could do their work more efficiently. Starting in the 1880s, manufacturers hired efficiency experts to cut down the amount of effort it took to build things in factories. The experts' recommendations eventually led to the creation of the assembly line, in which each worker had a specific job and all the equipment he needed was at his or her workstation. Other businesses hired efficiency experts to speed up record keeping, bill collecting, and all the other paperwork tasks that were draining time and money away from the business day. These systematizers recommended that their clients install the latest adding machines and typewriters, as part of getting ready to do business in the 20th century.

The office machine companies helped make the transition easy for their prospective customers. Since few people could learn how to use a keyboard on their own, Remington, Felt and Tarrant, and other firms opened training centers in large cities to teach clerks—as well as young men and women who wanted to find office work—how to operate their desktop machines. Stores that sold the new devices also housed repair centers for equipment that broke under the pressure of daily office use. And the manufacturers began tailoring their products to the wide range of customers they wanted to reach—"One Built for Every Line of Business," as the Burroughs Adding Machine Company said in a 1907 advertisement that promoted the 58 different calculators the firm made.

Early Excursions into Cybernetics

Many people refer to the final two decades of the 20th century, and at least the first few years of the 21st century, as the information age. The information age began, more or less, with the appearance of desktop computers in offices in the late 1970s and the personal computer boom of the 1980s. The rapid rise of the Internet and the World Wide Web in the 1990s solidified the idea of information as a valuable commodity, especially when businesses began using these networks for such tasks as online banking or transferring clothing designs to overseas factories.

Office machines and other technological advances had a similar effect during the 20th century's first two decades. In addition to typewriters and calculators, people and businesses were beginning to see the advantages of telephones, wireless telegraphs, automobiles, and airplanes, all of which made the tasks of handling information and transferring it to other people both faster and easier.

The punch-card tabulator developed into an important tool of this faster age. In the early 1900s Hollerith developed a more advanced version of the machine used in the 1890 census, one that automatically performed the tasks of reading and sorting punch cards. Hollerith's customers, mostly big businesses and government agencies, used their machines to calculate operating costs, order supplies, analyze sales figures, and take care of other tasks that that were, and still are, vital to their operations.

In 1911 Hollerith's Tabulating Machine Company merged with two other equipment companies, one that made time clocks and another that made scales; together, the three businesses became the Computing-Tabulating-Recording Company, or C-T-R. For its general manager, the new company hired Thomas J. Watson Sr., a former sales manager for the National Cash Register Company.

National Cash Register had been in business since 1884, when a businessman named John Patterson bought the rights to manufacture a cash register invented by James Ritty, a restaurant owner who thought his employees were stealing money from the till. Ritty's Incorruptible Cashier recorded each day's sales on a roll of paper inside the machine, where his employees could not get to it. By comparing the money in the cash drawer with the sales total from the register, Ritty was able to figure out if his staff was as honest as they claimed to be.

John Patterson—who was Ritty's sole customer when the restaurant owner tried to cash in on his invention—knew that the machine could be a big seller if it was marketed correctly, and if its design kept improving over the years. Patterson did two things that would be repeated by many successful companies in decades to come. He hired and trained a team of professional salesmen who were able to show storekeepers how a cash register could improve their business, and he established a research and development division that he called his "inventions department" to produce new models.

Watson borrowed and improved upon these two business innovations when he took over as president of C-T-R. Until that time, most of C-T-R's sales came from the division that made time clocks for factories. However, Watson realized that the tabulating machines held the biggest potential for future growth, and he slowly shifted the company's focus onto the information processing machines.

Two years before Watson became C-T-R's president, a rival company, the Powers Accounting Machine Company, had begun selling a punch-card-based tabulation system of its own. The Powers machines performed much the same as the machines C-T-R sold, with one difference: they printed out the results of their work. To regain a competitive edge, Watson started a research and development division within C-T-R and ordered it to make the necessary improvements.

Watson also changed how the C-T-R tabulator salesmen did their work. Even after Hollerith left the company, C-T-R continued his policy of leasing tabulator equipment rather than selling them. The first two or three years of the lease paid for the cost of building and maintaining the equipment; after that, all the money that came in was profit. The company also was the only reliable source for punch cards its customers had; cards from other sources caused the machines to seize up.

Leasing products instead of selling them outright is a tricky proposition. C-T-R was charging for the right to use its equipment, not for ownership of the machines. Watson's salesmen had to show their customers that the advantages to using C-T-R machines, rather than their competitor's, were worth the cost. To make that happen, the salesmen had to apply the skills of the efficiency expert; they learned how to analyze a prospective customer's accounting and record-keeping methods and pinpoint ways in which C-T-R equipment could increase efficiency. The exact nature of the information was unimportant; all that the salesmen had to do was figure the path this information took through a company and work out a better way of handling it.

In a way, by analyzing how a customer's billing operations could be improved with their machines, Watson and his salesmen were pioneers in the field of cybernetics. An American mathematician, Norbert Weiner, coined the term *cybernetics* in 1948 to describe a newly emerging science of how information is transmitted and organized, whether in mechanical machines such as computers or in organic structures such as the human nervous system. The word *cybernetics* comes from the Greek word *kybernetes*, or steersman, referring to the sailor who controls a ship's rudder and thus maneuvers it across the waves. Because complex machines like tabulation systems helped determine how information was maneuvered through a company, they are forerunners to the business computers that would appear in the 1950s and to the supercomputers that would be developed afterward.

ARTILLERY TABLES AND CODE BREAKERS

Office machines made work much easier for the human computers who tallied lists of sales, expense reports, and other business-related numbers. Using this equipment for scientific and other nonfinancial calculations was a different matter. The machines that were good for simple arithmetic generally were not able to handle tasks that required high-level mathematics, and attempts to link calculators together usually failed to work.

One exception to this rule took place at Great Britain's Nautical Almanac Office, where an astronomer named Leslie John Comrie abolished the old system of using freelance human computers in 1925. For the more simple calculations, ones that involved only basic math, Comrie hired young women who were adept at using adding machines. A more complicated navigation table, one showing the position of the Moon throughout the year, was handled differently. Comrie set up an IBM punch-card calculator that in less than seven months printed out 20 years' worth of Moon-position tables, drastically cutting the cost to the *Nautical Almanac*'s publishers.

As successful as it was, Comrie's adaptation of mechanical calculators to science shows why scientists usually did not use office machines in their work. The Almanac Office's staff had to create a set of more than 500,000 punch cards containing the information and operating instructions needed to run the IBM calculator. This step alone took months. Then, while the tables were being calculated, the machine's operators had to feed these cards back into the machine's card reader. Otherwise, when the last card went through, the machine would stop; it was not designed to continue its work automatically.

In the early 1930s, Vannevar Bush, an engineering professor at the Massachusetts Institute of Technology, built a machine that resolved these problems, at least for a short time. Bush's invention was the differential analyzer, an electrically powered mechanical calculator that used gear wheels and spinning metal shafts to come up with answers to a type of math problem called a differential equation. Calculating with this type of mechanism is called *analog* calculation. Rather than calculating with precisely defined numerical values, analog machines like the differential analyzer draw patterns of changes in equations.

Scientists and engineers use differential equations to analyze how friction, gravity, and other forces influence moving objects. These forces can work with or against each other, and their effects can grow or decrease in strength as objects move. Differential equations take all of these variations into account, and thus are very difficult to solve. With changes to the arrangement of the gears and gear shafts, Bush's device could analyze a wide range of engineering and scientific phenomena.

The differential analyzer was not a computer, but it was the most advanced calculator of its type that had been invented. Even so, it was difficult to operate: it could take a couple of days to change the configuration of its inner workings, and its operators constantly had to make small adjustments to its mechanism while it was working. Despite these drawbacks, research centers deeply desired to have an analyzer of their own, and a few models went into service at universities and nonacademic labs in the United States, England, and Norway.

Number Crunching for the Military

One of the sites that got a differential analyzer in the late 1930s, the U.S. Army's Aberdeen Proving Ground in Maryland, was very happy to have it. The Aberdeen Proving Ground was where army artillery pieces—from howitzers to long-range guns—were tested for accuracy.

More important, the facility was home to the army's Ballistics Research Laboratory, where firing tables for each type of gun were made.

Soldiers have a nickname for artillery: They call it "the king of battle," because, like a king on a chessboard, artillery forces move slowly but wield great power. Once an artillery battery gets into position, it can saturate an area with exploding shells and other ordnance, "softening it up" for an attack by infantry or tank forces. Aiming an artillery piece, however, is not simple. A shell's trajectory—the path it takes through the air from gun to target—is influenced by more than the charge of gunpowder that shoots it from the barrel. Air temperature, wind, the type of ground on which the gun is sitting—these and many other variables affect where and how the shell might travel.

It would take far too long and waste too much ammunition for gun crews to adjust the trajectories from scratch each time they went into combat. Instead, they use tables of standard trajectories that are computed specifically for each area where they are sent to fight. Until Bush invented his differential analyzer, trajectory tables were created just like many other numerical tables. Teams of human computers calculated all the potential trajectories for each type of gun, accounting for all the variables by hand and, later, by using desktop calculators. This task was one of the most difficult feats of mathematics that human beings were asked to perform. For each gun, teams of computers had to spend two or three months calculating the thousands of trajectories gun crews required.

The differential analyzer helped speed up this chore. Using their machine, and one at the nearby University of Pennsylvania, the Ballistics Research Laboratory was able to compute the basic trajectories of each gun, using just the data for a target's altitude and range, in less than three hours. Human computers took this data and adjusted it for the other variables, each person completing a full trajectory plot in roughly three days. This still was a slow method, but nothing faster was available, nor would anything faster even be suggested for at least four years.

IBM's Mark I and II

In 1937, about the time Bush's differential analyzers were being built and installed in their new homes, another university researcher came up with a proposal for a different type of differential analyzer. Howard Aiken was a mathematics professor at Harvard University who, like Bush, was seeking a way to speed up the drudgery of calculating dif-

IBM's Automatic Sequence Controlled Calculator, also known as the Harvard Mark I, impressed the public as much for its design as for the calculating abilities of its 3,300 mechanical relays. [Courtesy IBM Archives]

ferential equations. Because he was not an engineer, Aiken did not design the machine he had in mind, which he called the Automatic Sequence-Controlled Calculator (ASCC). Instead, he wrote a detailed description of what the machine should be able to do and described his general view of how it should be built.

The ASCC should, Aiken wrote, be automatic, in the sense that it would be able to calculate without any assistance from a human operator, aside from the task of entering data. And its operation should be controlled by a sequence of commands that was entered along with the data and told the calculator what to do with the information. (Today, computers store programs such as these in their temporary memories; there was no comparable way to store such information in a strictly mechanical device like the ASCC.)

Aiken attempted to get Harvard's physics department to turn his idea into a working machine, but he was turned down. Next, he contacted the nearby Monroe Calculating Machine Company, one of the nation's larger office machine manufacturers, thinking the company's managers would be eager to develop a machine like the ASCC. Unfortunately, Monroe's executives were not interested in building a machine that had only science and engineering applications.

Finally, in 1938, Aiken went to IBM. Just before this last attempt, though, Aiken learned that a tiny portion of Babbage's Analytical Engine was sitting in the attic of Harvard's physics building. No more than a few of the engine's gears mounted on rods that were fixed to a small wooden base, the section was a gift that Babbage's son made to Harvard in 1886 for the university's 250th birthday. To Aiken, the small collection of parts was a sign that he was on the right track, and he researched Babbage's work to see what other inspiration he could gain. Aiken mentioned Babbage's work and his goals for the Analytical Engine in a rewritten proposal for the ASCC.

Fortunately for Aiken, Thomas Watson still was president of IBM and had been supporting research into scientific uses for his company's machines. He decided that Aiken's proposal was worth supporting, and in 1939 IBM's board of directors approved the project and its $100,000 budget (almost $1.3 million in 2003 money). A team of company engineers began turning Aiken's proposal into a working machine, with Aiken serving as a consultant on the project.

The Harvard-IBM Automatic Sequence-Controlled Calculator Mark I, as the calculator was renamed, was ready for its first test run in 1943. However, those tests were conducted in secret. By 1943, the United States had been fighting in World War II for more than a year and the U.S. Navy had taken over control of the Mark I for use during wartime. Aiken, now a junior officer in the navy, was put in charge of the machine, which he formally presented to the public in 1944.

What the IBM engineers built from Aiken's proposal came close to being a true computer. As Aiken had wanted, the machine was automatic, receiving its data and instructions from a three-inch-wide punch tape. An electric motor turned a 50-foot-long drive shaft that sent the five-ton mechanism into action. All along the eight-foot-high, 51-foot-long, two-foot-thick machine, number wheels turned in the sequence demanded by the punch-tape program, making a clattering racket that sounded to a scientist who saw the Mark I in motion like "a roomful of ladies knitting." The results of the clicking calculations were recorded on IBM punch cards, which were deciphered using a separate printer.

Two things keep the Mark I from being considered a computer. First, it had no way to store a program that it read from a punch tape. A few basic operations that were permanently wired into a series of control circuits, but those could not be changed any more than the circuits in a pocket calculator can be changed. In general, the Mark I only worked as long as a punch tape was running though its reader; for extended calculations, the ends of a tape could be glued together to make an unending belt of instructions.

The second obstacle was the Mark I's inability to use the results of its computations to adjust the program it was following, something known as a conditional branch or an "if-then" jump. Basically, conditional branches are what allow computers to act as computers, giving users the ability to interact with their machines and letting computers adjust how information flows through their circuitry. The only thing the IBM engineers designed their calculator to do was follow the instructions on its punch tape or in its permanent circuits.

These problems aside, the Mark I was an impressive piece of machinery, especially after Watson hired an industrial designer who gave it a streamlined, steel-and-glass exterior. Unfortunately, during its unveiling ceremony, Aiken neglected to mention the work done by IBM's engineers—giving the impression that he alone had designed the Mark I—or the fact that IBM had financed the machine's construction. Enraged, Watson abandoned any further work with the Harvard professor and ordered his chief engineers to build a calculator that worked faster and did more than Aiken's.

The navy used the Mark I and a second Aiken-designed machine called the Mark II to calculate mathematics tables. Aiken would build two more calculators, the Mark III and Mark IV, in the late 1940s and 1950s, but these machines were the final examples of an old way of crunching numbers.

A Colossal Advance in Cracking an Enigma

In September 1939, soldiers of Nazi Germany invaded Poland, forcing Great Britain and France to declare war and thus starting World War II. Right from the start, the other nations of Europe were in trouble. Under Adolf Hitler, Germany had been building one of the world's most powerful and well-equipped military forces. Within nine months, Germany conquered Poland, Denmark, Norway, the Netherlands, Belgium, Luxembourg, and France; more than 300,000 British and French troops were forced to flee across the English Channel to Britain, leaving weapons and equipment behind.

Much of Germany's success early in the war came from its use of two supposedly unbreakable codes to send orders to its armed forces. The most-used code was created with a machine called the Enigma, a word that means "mystery" or "puzzle." The Enigma looked like a box-shaped typewriter, with a keyboard in the front and a set of illuminated letters on top of the box. When an operator pushed one of the keys, a different letter would light up (numbers were spelled out). Constantly changing electrical circuits determined which letter would light up; the circuits ran through three or four rotating disks that changed position each time a key was pressed. The starting point for the rotors was changed each day, according to a top-secret schedule. In addition to the rotors, a secondary electric circuit board beneath the keyboard allowed the Enigma operator to further alter the circuit path from the keys to the lighted letters. Altogether, the machine could create trillions of possible circuits, making Enigma an almost perfect randomizer. No one who used the machine thought its code ever could be broken.

The other encryption method was called the Lorenz cipher, named for the company that developed it for the German army's high command. The Lorenz cipher machine translated the text of a message into a string of meaningless characters; the message then was transmitted to its destination, where another cipher machine decoded it. Unlike the 26-letter Enigma machine, the Lorenz machine used a 32-symbol code, with one symbol for each letter and six other symbols indicating spaces between sentences, divisions between paragraphs, and similar information.

With these two codes, Germany organized air strikes, troop movements, and submarine attacks on commercial shipping without worrying if orders might be intercepted. For England, decoding the German radio signals became one of the most important tasks of the war. In 1938 the British government realized Britain might have to go to war with Germany and set up a secret code-breaking project to decipher the Enigma messages. After the war started, the project was moved to an estate north of London called Bletchley Park. The project hired mathematicians, language experts, crossword-puzzle hobbyists, and anyone else who might have the knowledge it would take to crack Enigma and, later, the Lorenz code, to which the British assigned the code-name FISH.

Alan Turing, a mathematical genius who joined the code breakers in 1938, took charge of a group that was trying to decipher a version of the Enigma code used by the German navy. The naval version was harder to crack—its Enigmas used an extra rotor to complete the encoding circuits, adding an extra level of randomness to the code.

The goal of breaking the supposedly indecipherable codes generated by the Enigma machine led to the creation of two computers at Great Britain's Bletchley Park cryptography center. (Courtesy of the National Security Agency)

Fortunately, a group of Polish mathematicians had worked out a method to decipher codes made using an earlier version of Enigma, and they were able to pass this information to the British before the war started. Also, a captured German submarine yielded a copy of the naval Enigma codebook with the initial setting for the rotors. Using the clues these documents provided, in 1940 Turing and his team built an electromechanical decryption machine they called a "bombe." The bombe allowed Turing's staff to test different possible code combinations, eliminate combinations that obviously were wrong, and come up with a series of possible correct translations that other code breakers worked on by hand. By the end of the war, Bletchley Park was using bombes to read the German military's mail.

Identifying the FISH code actually took less time than it took to decode the Enigma. When British listening posts first picked up radio signals sent using FISH in 1940, a top-ranking British army code expert recognized the pattern of the symbols and the code they represented. Recognizing the method did not mean the code was cracked, however. The Bletchley Park team only managed to decode small

Programmed with punched tape, seen in the rear of this photograph, Colossus was one of the world's first working electronic computers. Its job was to decipher German military codes during World War II. [© Public Record Office/Topham-HIP/The Image Works]

fragments of the FISH transmissions until, by a stroke of luck, they picked up a 4,000-word message that a German operator sent twice with slight changes in the text. This mistake gave the code-breakers enough information about the code to work out a key to solving it.

To speed up the process of deciphering the FISH code, a mathematician named Max Newmann and an electronics engineer named Tommy Flowers designed a machine to automatically scan a punch tape version of an intercepted message and decode it. The machine, which was named Colossus, used 1,500 vacuum tubes in the circuits that calculated how the Lorenz machine had encoded the message. The time needed to decode a FISH message went from a maximum of six weeks to just a few hours.

Ten Colossus machines and 12 bombes were built during the war. When the conflict was over, however, all but two Colossus calculators and all the bombes were dismantled, to ensure the secrecy of the operation. (The remaining two Colossus machines were destroyed in the 1960s, along with most of their design plans.)

THE FIRST "THINKING MACHINES"

At the beginning of 1942, while Britain's code breakers were fighting their battles against Enigma, the United States was trying, among other things, to get its artillery tables in order.

America's armed forces knew that winning World War II was going to be their biggest task ever, considering that the United States was facing war on two fronts. The Pacific Ocean was the theater of operations for an island-hopping campaign against the military of imperial Japan; on the other side of the world, Americans joined British and European armies to face down the combined troops of Nazi Germany and Fascist Italy. The battlefields would include the deserts of North Africa, the mountains of mainland Europe, and the jungles of the South Pacific.

These changes in climate and terrain posed special challenges for U.S. Army artillery units. In World War I the United States had fought in fewer nations, and then only in Europe. All new tables had to be calculated not just for old guns left over from World War I but also for new guns whose designs had not been tested in action. The human computers working at the army's Ballistics Research Laboratory were able to keep up with the demand at first. Though they had to do most of their work using only a desk calculator, they were able to finish a gun's trajectory table in about two months. In 1943, however, they began to lose ground against the hundreds of orders that were pouring into the laboratory's Aberdeen, Maryland, offices. The "kings of battle" were being asked to rule over unfamiliar kingdoms, but their crews lacked the manuals that described how the kings should wield their power. Then a solution seemed to present itself, when two researcher-engineers from Pennsylvania asked the army to pay for a calculator that used electricity in place of gear shafts.

A Room Full of Vacuum Tubes

The two researchers, Dr. John Mauchly and a graduate student named J. Presper Eckert, worked in the University of Pennsylvania's Moore School of Engineering in Philadelphia. They met in 1941, when Mauchly attended a special summer course at the university on designing electronic systems for military use. Though he had just received his bachelor's degree that spring, Eckert was assigned to serve as Mauchly's laboratory instructor. The two men turned out to have similar interests in building electronic equipment, and both wanted to create an all-electronic calculator.

After Mauchly completed his coursework, the Moore School hired him as a full-time professor, and he and Eckert began designing a calculator that would replace the differential analyzer and its dependence on analog methods. Their machine would use a series of on-off switches to solve equations using decimal math, with circuit boards that registered numbers from 0 to 9. It would not use electromechanical relays like those in Howard Aiken's Mark I calculator, however, even though the relays had proven reliable. Relays were slow, and the Moore engineers wanted their machine to be the fastest calculator on the planet. The only way to meet this goal was with electrical circuits that solved equations directly.

Mauchly already had seen such a device at work that summer, at the Iowa State University laboratory of electrical engineering run by Professor John V. Atanasoff. With the help of a graduate student named Clifford Berry, Atanasoff built a digital electronic calculator that could solve equations using electric circuits in place of gears and camshafts. The heart of the machine was a bank of 210 vacuum tubes—glass tubes that look like long, clear light bulbs containing a few rows of wire filaments—that did most of the work. Another bank of 30 tubes controlled a punch card reader and recorder, while a third group of tubes regulated power flowing to a simple, drum-shaped memory system.

Scientists had worked with vacuum tubes to explore and harness the power of electricity since the middle of the 19th century; the lightbulb invented by Thomas Edison in 1879 was a globe-shaped vacuum tube that contained a single wire filament. Why use a vacuum? Simple: As electricity passes through the wire in a vacuum tube, the wire heats up. In a vacuum the wire can get very hot and stay that way for a long time before it melts. In the presence of oxygen, however, the wire burns out instantly, if it is thin enough and enough power is flowing through it.

Vacuum tubes of the type Atanasoff used were first developed in 1904 for radios, wireless telegraphs, and other communication devices. (Decades later, vacuum tubes were also used in the circuits of television sets.) The tubes acted mainly as amplifiers that could enhance weak signals and modulators that controlled the amount of electricity flowing through the circuits. Some scientists experimented with other ways to use vacuum tubes, including two British scientists who came up with a way to use vacuum tubes in a simple on-off circuit known as a "flip-flop." When the circuit was turned on, one tube would be on while the other tube would be off. At the push of a button or with some other signal, the "off" tube would flip on while the "on" tube flopped off.

(Actually, "on" and "off" are just shorthand ways to describe what really happens in a circuit such as this. Unlike a lightbulb, a vacuum tube's filaments have to be warm before they can work, and it takes too long to warm up a cold tube. To get around this limitation, vacuum tubes are designed to operate with high ("on") or low ("off") amounts of electricity flowing through them.)

Though it was only half finished when Mauchly saw it and never worked as successfully as Atanasoff had hoped it would, the calculator—eventually named the Atanasoff-Berry Computer—was a significant milestone in the history of computing. It was the first machine to use vacuum tubes to calculate mathematical equations and the first electronic machine to use binary numbers. It was not a true computer. It could not store a program, it was not automatic (someone had to be in charge of the machine while it was calculating), and it was restricted to only one type of mathematical operation. However, it clearly showed that computing with vacuum tubes was faster than using any electromechanical substitute.

The machine that Mauchly and Eckert came up with after nearly a year of discussion was not really a computer in the modern sense, either.

It was an electronic version of a differential analyzer, a big calculator that could work faster and provide greater accuracy than the mechanical, analog machines being used. In August 1942 they wrote a letter to the Moore School's dean and research director, describing their concept and asking for support from the school to build it. Unfortunately, every other calculator research project in the nation was focused on improv-

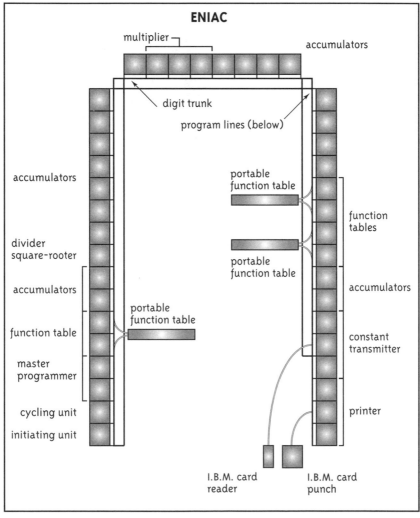

This diagram shows the room-filling layout of ENIAC. Technicians could place the three moveable function tables in various locations around the room, depending on the task on which they were working.

ing analog calculations, and the university officials rejected the proposal as being too impractical and unlikely to succeed.

Eight months later, in April 1943, Mauchly and Eckert had a second chance to build their electronic calculator. An army officer with a doctorate in mathematics happened to hear from a University of Pennsylvania engineering student about the proposal that the university had turned down. It was a fortunate conversation for the officer, Lt. Herman Goldstine, who had been assigned to the Ballistics Research Laboratory in Maryland with orders to solve the artillery table problem by any means possible. Mauchly and Eckert's project, he decided, fit his orders exactly, and he set up a meeting with the researchers and a panel made up of his superiors and a selection of technical experts.

The army panel took less time to approve the project than it took Goldstine, Mauchly, and Eckert (along with a member of the Moore School administration) to drive from Philadelphia to the Aberdeen,

Historians consider ENIAC, the Electronic Numeric Integrator and Calculator, to be the first working general-purpose electronic computer. Its inventors built it for the U.S. Army, which used it to calculate firing tables. [Courtesy U.S. Army Research Laboratory, Aberdeen Proving Ground, Maryland]

Maryland, army base. The project was designated "Project PX" and classified top secret, but eventually it became known by the name Mauchly and Eckert gave it: the Electronic Numerical Integrator and Calculator, or ENIAC.

Unfortunately for the Ballistic Research Laboratory's overworked human computers, ENIAC was not finished in time to help them with their wartime calculations. Work began on ENIAC in the early summer of 1943 at the Moore School; the machine was ready to run by the end of 1945. World War II ended in August 1945 with the surrender of Japan (Germany had surrendered the previous spring). Still, there was plenty of work to do to prepare for the coming cold war with the communist Union of Soviet Socialist Republics, and ENIAC was put to work.

ENIAC was a titanic machine, taking up a 1,800-square-foot room at the University of Pennsylvania; it had to be, to house the 18,000 vacuum tubes that allowed it to work. Eighty feet long and eight feet high, the calculator was made up of 40 cabinets filled with electronic circuitry that—together with the wires that connected its various components, a set of three movable special-function tables, a punch card reader and a card puncher—weighed 30 tons. It could compute the trajectory of an artillery shell in only 20 seconds; shells usually took a full 30 seconds to reach their targets. Once, when ENIAC was programmed to solve a difficult equation that required 15 million multiplications, it completed the task in only one weekend. The same work, if done by a single human computer using a desktop calculator, would have taken 40 years.

Setting the Pattern for Future Computers

ENIAC was not without its problems. Its power-hungry vacuum tubes generated a tremendous amount of heat, and even more power had to be used to run a series of fans to carry this heat away. When some of the tubes failed, the computer could not be used until troubleshooters located and replaced them, a task that was both costly and time consuming. Of course, using the machine even at the best of times was a time-consuming task, as the entire room-sized mechanism had to be rewired for each calculating run. It took technicians the better part of two full days to program ENIAC to solve an equation, setting thousands of switches and connecting the hundreds of wire cables that allowed the components of ENIAC to "talk" to one another. Then a set of punch cards containing the initial data had to be entered into the reader. When ENIAC finished its work, it printed the results on another set of cards that were deciphered on a separate machine.

There were other limitations to ENIAC's design. Because it was rewired for each calculation, it could not store programs for later use. The vacuum-tube circuit boards within ENIAC could not store numbers that were longer than 10 digits, and they could only handle 20 of those numbers at a time. For the machine to run through an entire series of calculations, it had to print out punch cards each time it reached its limit; those cards were fed back into the machine until the job was completed.

But its drawbacks were overshadowed by the fact that, for the first time in history, there was an all-electronic machine that could solve complicated math equations. More important, ENIAC was a general-purpose machine, one that had been designed for any type of mathematical work; this feature separated it from Atanasoff's computer, which had been designed for just one type of algebraic calculation. News reports of ENIAC's official unveiling in 1946 marveled at how it worked "faster than thought" and proclaimed that its creation had ushered in the era of thinking machines. ENIAC was moved to Aberdeen, where it ran the numbers for hydrogen bomb tests, missile and wind tunnel designs, and other projects (including artillery tables) until 1955.

Many historians view the creation of ENIAC as the beginning of the computer age, the point at which digital technology began to replace analog systems. At the time, however, Mauchly and Eckert knew that the words of praise from the press were a bit more than ENIAC deserved, considering its limitations. By the time ENIAC was switched on, the two engineers had come up with a design for its successor, one that solved most of the problems with ENIAC's design and used far fewer vacuum tubes and other components. Once again, the army approved the construction of a Mauchly/Eckert math machine: this one was the Electronic Discrete Variable Calculator, or EDVAC.

The design of EDVAC marked the first use of the stored-program concept in electronic computing. A stored-program computer is one in which the instructions that tell the machine what to do are loaded directly into its memory. Unlike ENIAC, which had to be rewired for each type of calculation, a stored-program computer never needs to have its circuits changed. Mauchly and Eckert realized that this way of building computers would make EDVAC faster than ENIAC, as

EDVAC would take less time to program and would be able to act on its instructions more rapidly.

The engineers also designed EDVAC to be smaller than ENIAC. In all, EDVAC used only 8,000 vacuum tubes, compared to the 18,000 used by ENIAC. The reduction was the result of using a memory circuit Eckert had designed called the mercury delay line—a tube filled with liquid mercury that stored information in the form of electronic pulses that ran from one end of the tube to the other until the computer needed it. This and other innovative elements of EDVAC's design helped set the standard for other computers.

In a weird twist of fate, though, Eckert and Mauchly failed to receive recognition as the ones who devised the delay line, the stored-program concept, and EDVAC itself. In fall 1944, one of the 20th century's most famous mathematicians, John Von Neumann, visited the Moore School at the request of Herman Goldstine, the army officer who was supervising ENIAC's construction. Von Neumann became interested in ENIAC and helped its designers solve a few problems with its design. Naturally, he became interested in the design of EDVAC, and helped the Moore School engineers design part of that computer as well.

Then, in 1945, Von Neumann wrote a paper called "First Draft of a Report on the EDVAC," in which he described how and why the computer was being built. As the title suggested, the paper was not meant to be the final word on EDVAC's creation and design; in fact, Von Neumann and Goldstine (whom the army had put in charge of EDVAC) saw it simply as a reference tool for the people working on EDVAC. However, the report found its way to colleagues of Von Neumann's in America and England, and those colleagues sent copies of it to other scholars and engineers.

The unintended distribution of the paper created problems for Mauchly and Eckert. In the world of academics and research, the first person or group of people to write about a phenomenon or an invention generally are the ones who are given credit for its discovery. Unfortunately, the "first draft" carried only Von Neumann's name as its author; in it, the mathematician mentioned Mauchly by name only once and did not mention Eckert at all. Most people who read it got the impression that Von Neumann had come up with the idea for the stored-program computer. Mauchly and Eckert tried to counteract this impression with a paper of their own, but it was never distributed as widely as Von Neumann's.

Because of this mistaken understanding, the type of stored-program computer design that EDVAC represented became known as the

Von Neumann architecture (the word *architecture* meaning "method of construction").

EDSAC, UNIVAC, and Other First-Generation Computers

As things turned out, EDVAC, which was the first stored-program electronic computer, was not even one of the first five stored-program electronic computers to be built. After ENIAC's "grand opening," Mauchly and Eckert fought with the University of Pennsylvania over who held patent rights to their work. The two men quit their positions at the Moore School, and the EDVAC project effectively ceased to exist for a few years. In the meantime, British scientists who read Von Neumann's paper decided to tackle the construction of a stored-program computer, using the mathematician's description of EDVAC as their guide. Alan Turing, who had supervised the Bletchley Park code-

Britain's EDSAC, the Electronic Delay Storage Automated Computer, was the second electronic stored-program computer to become operational. [© Computer Laboratory, University of Cambridge, U.K. Reproduced by permission.]

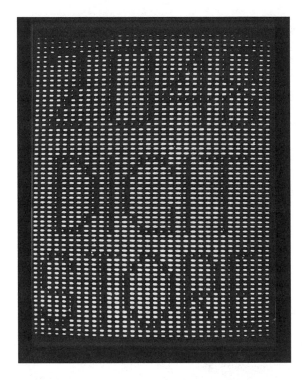

An interesting method for storing data was to use cathode-ray tubes—like those used in televisions and computer monitors today—as the core components of computer memory. [Reproduced with permission of the Department of Computer Science, University of Manchester, U.K.]

breaking program, drew up plans for an EDVAC-style machine at the request of Britain's National Physical Laboratory. Turing called his creation the Automatic Computing Engine, or ACE, in honor of Charles Babbage's Difference and Analytical Engines. Like Babbage's engines, unfortunately, the ACE was never built—problems created by the government blocked construction—though a smaller version, the Pilot ACE, was assembled in 1950.

In 1948 scientists at Britain's Manchester University succeeded where the National Physical Laboratory had failed. The Manchester Mark I computer was different from EDVAC's design in one important way: instead of a mercury delay line, the Mark I used cathode-ray tubes, like the tubes used in television sets, to store information. A cathode-ray tube, or CRT, uses a beam of electrons to paint images on the inside surface of its screen. The Manchester University scientists figured a way to make the electron beams write and read bits of information instead. This technological trick helped the Manchester Mark I become the world's first operational, fully electronic stored-program computer. The system worked well enough that a commercial electronics firm in Manchester, with help from the British government, began building similar computers and selling them to universities and government agencies.

EDSAC, the Electronic Delay Storage Automated Computer, was the second electronic stored-program computer to become operational. It was based on the Von Neumann architecture of EDVAC, down to its mercury delay-line memory. Built at Cambridge University in 1949, EDSAC actually was more powerful than the Manchester Mark I and other CRT computers. Although slower than CRT memory, the delay line held more information and was more reliable than the CRTs, which occasionally lost some of the data that was printed on their screens.

Nineteen forty-nine also was the year that a stored-program computer began operating in the United States. After leaving the Moore School of Engineering, Mauchly and Eckert formed America's first computer company, the Electronic Control Corporation (which they later renamed the Eckert-Mauchly Computer Corporation). They

In one of the earliest public demonstrations of digital computing power, UNIVAC predicted the outcome of the 1952 presidential race. Here, UNIVAC cocreator J. Presper Eckert (center) and reporter Walter Cronkite (right) examine results of the computer's calculations as a technician looks on. [Courtesy Unisys Corp.]

wanted to build not just a single computer but a general-purpose data processing system that could store information on magnetic tape, process bills for large corporations, handle scientific calculations, and even print out the results of its work in plain English. It would be a universal automatic computer; in fact, it would be *the* Universal Automatic Computer, or UNIVAC.

In a repetition of history, the Census Bureau was to have the first UNIVAC to come out of the Electronic Control Corporation's workshop. To bring in extra money, the Electronic Control Company also signed a contract to build a smaller computer called the Binary Automatic Computer, or BINAC, for the Northrop Aircraft Company, which wanted to develop a computerized airborne navigation system. BINAC, then, became the computer that brought the stored-program concept to reality in America.

Other companies soon joined in the race to build computers over the next decade, whether by developing machines of their own or by purchasing a company whose desire to build computers was undercut by bad business sense. Sadly, the Eckert-Mauchly Computer Corporation was one of these companies. Neither BINAC nor the first UNIVAC contracts were moneymakers, and the pioneering computer scientists sold the firm to business machine manufacturer Remington Rand in 1950. After the sale, though, UNIVAC became one of the great commercial successes of the early computer age, especially when it was used successfully to predict the outcome of the 1952 presidential election.

This first group, or first generation, of computers all had one thing in common: vacuum tubes. Though mercury lines and cathode-ray tubes were used to store information, and the machines were far smaller than Colossus or ENIAC, there was no practical substitute available for vacuum tubes during the first decade of the computing age. However, scientists were working on something that eventually replaced vacuum tubes in all but a few electronic devices.

SMALLER IS BIGGER

In a way, each of the computers built in the 10 years after ENIAC's debut can be seen as a supercomputer, as each new computer was faster and more powerful than its predecessor. By the time a new computer went into operation, other computer scientists and manufacturers were working on better electronic "brains." And as they tested their new machines, the designers discovered ways to make computers that were even better.

On the other hand, these early computers shared one drawback. The weakest links in their electronic circuits were the big, space-consuming vacuum tubes that stored and processed information. Reducing the number of these hot, fragile, and power-hungry parts became one of the most important goals of computer design. Even when engineers copied the idea of the Manchester Mark I computer, with its CRT-based memory, they only solved part of the problem. CRTs were far bulkier than vacuum tubes and were power-hungry in their own right. Plus, they were not suited for data processing, which required components that could switch on and off far more rapidly than the dots on a CRT screen could.

The search for smaller alternatives to computer vacuum tubes began soon after World War II, and it yielded results before the end of the 1940s. In 1949 an engineer at MIT, Jay Forrester, came up with a circuit that could replace many of a computer's vacuum tubes. Forrester developed a form of memory that stored information on tiny magnetic rings mounted on a grid of electric wires. Three wires passed through the center of each ring; passing a small charge of electricity through two of these wires caused the ring's magnetic field to flip over, with the north and south poles changing position. This shift in polarity served the same function as the "on-off" settings of a vacuum tube. The third wire passing through the ring allowed the computer to read the ring's polarity. Called magnetic-core memory, Forrester's component led to a great leap upward in speed and reliability, while reducing both the amount of maintenance and the amount of floor space that a computer required.

Unfortunately, the other problem remained. As with CRTs, magnetic cores were good for storing information but were not suited for the rapid work of information processing. Vacuum tubes were the only components fast enough to perform these calculations. Even so, the way forward was clear: the computers of the future would be faster, smaller, and able to handle increasingly complicated tasks. Room-filling computers still would exist, but they would be capable of far greater amounts of work than the 40 or so cabinets of ENIAC. All that computer scientists needed in order to bring about this future technology was a way to replace the vacuum tubes that formed the heart of computer circuitry.

Transistors Take to the Field

The component that would replace vacuum tubes came from a group of scientists at Bell Telephone Laboratories, a famed research center operated by the Bell Systems telephone company. Starting in the late 1930s, the laboratory had been searching for a new type of telephone switching device that would be faster than an electromechanical relay and more reliable than a vacuum tube. The project focused on materials called semiconductors, elements and compounds that are somewhat resistant to the flow of electricity. Electrons pass through conductors, such as metal, much as water flows through a pipe or a garden hose. Insulators—such as rubber, glass, and wood—are impervious to the flow of electricity. A semiconductor, as its name implies, is somewhere in between, neither allowing nor stopping the flow of electricity entirely.

Throughout the 1940s Bell Labs scientists experimented with different methods for turning semiconductors into resilient switches with no moving parts, a type of circuitry that was to form the basis of solid-state electronics. Three researchers in particular—William Shockley, Walter Brattain, and John Bardeen—began working on ways to control how and when electricity flowed across a small slab of germanium, one of the most well-known semiconductors. In 1947 the researchers developed a device that seemed to offer what they sought. It blocked electric currents that were lower than a predetermined voltage (a volt

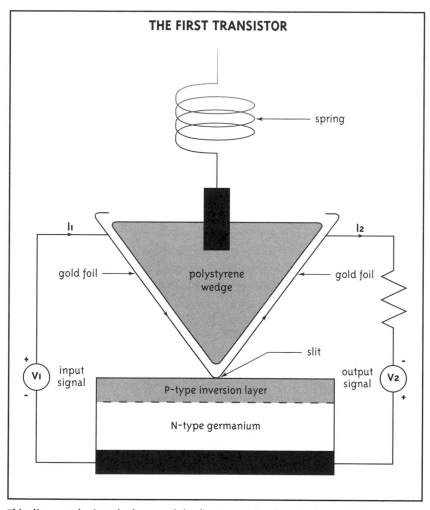

THE FIRST TRANSISTOR

spring

I₁

I₂

gold foil

polystyrene wedge

gold foil

slit

+
V₁   input signal

P-type inversion layer

N-type germanium

output signal   V₂

This diagram depicts the layout of the first transistor, invented at Bell Laboratories in the late 1940s. Called a point-contact transistor, the device led to the first wave of miniaturization in electronics, including computers.

is a measure of the force of an electric current) but allowed higher-voltage currents to pass through.

The crude device—which looked like a thick glass arrowhead connected to a couple of wires that pressed against the germanium slab—sent electrical pulses from an electrical emitter on one side of the arrowhead to a collector on the other. Because the device transferred electric charges across the resisting semiconductor, the new component was dubbed the transistor. Further work on the device led to a more sophisticated form of transistor that became the foundation for the solid-state switching system Bell Labs had been seeking.

The first of these improved electronic components was only about the size of a pencil eraser, and 200 of them could fit in the same space as one vacuum tube. They needed far less energy to operate than vacuum tubes required, and thus generated far less heat. Better still, transistors operated at significantly faster speeds than did electromechanical relays or vacuum tubes. The new switches even worked as soon as they were turned on; vacuum tubes needed to warm up for a few minutes before they were able to start shunting electricity through a system's circuits.

The three Bell Labs scientists won the Nobel Prize in physics in 1956 for their work, which sparked a revolution in electronics of all types, computers included. ENIAC, UNIVAC, and other *first-generation computers* (the ones that used vacuum tubes) were fast enough to perform from 1,000 to 5,000 additions per second. Computers built with transistors—the *second-generation computers*—could operate at speeds as high as 500,000 additions per second. It took the better part of a decade for transistors to become a standard component in computer circuitry, however. As with any new technological discovery, the process of making transistors had to be refined to the point where it was economical to manufacture the new components. And after that point was reached, transistors still needed to be wired by hand onto circuit boards. The wires that connected them were large and cumbersome in comparison to the size of the transistors, and the wire connections sometimes failed. It was not until the mid-to-late 1950s that transistors were ready to be used in the sensitive circuitry of computers.

About this time, another impetus began shaping the future of computers. In October 1957 the Soviet Union (USSR) launched the world's first artificial satellite, *Sputnik*, into orbit around the Earth. This event was a two-stage triumph for the Soviets: it established the USSR as a scientific and technological superpower, and it gave the communist state a technological edge over the democratic nations of Western Europe and North America. In particular, *Sputnik*'s voyage

SWITCHES

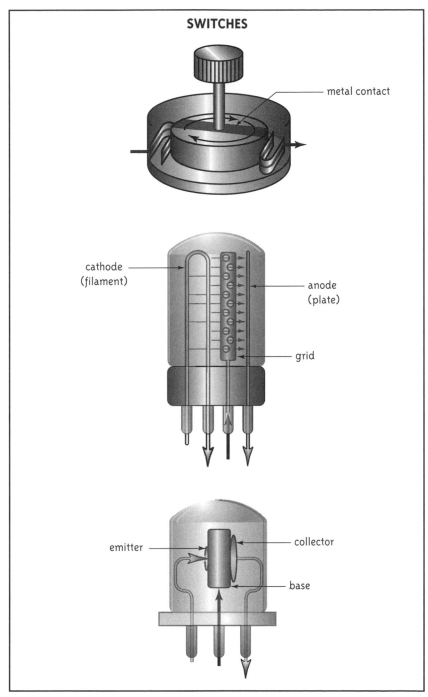

metal contact

cathode (filament)

anode (plate)

grid

emitter

collector

base

Whether mechanical (top), vacuum tube (middle), or transistor (bottom), switches have been the components that make computers able to compute since the 1940s. This illustration shows a side-by-side comparison of these types of switches.

sparked the so-called space race between the United States and the Soviets during the cold war. The United States was determined to regain technological superiority; to do so, it needed better computers.

Bringing Computers to the Business World

The computers that the United States had were already pretty good for their time, thanks in part to the military's investment in the technology. Until UNIVAC came on the market, most of the computers built after World War II were designed for military uses, such as atomic bomb calibrations and weapons control during missile launches. This was a natural development, considering that the people who designed these computers had worked on military projects during the war. ENIAC and Colossus were the best known of these machines, but there had been a few other projects to develop code breakers and calculators during World War II. Right after the end of the war, many of the people who did this pioneering work, both in America and Britain, formed computer-manufacturing companies and began developing computers for the military. A few other government agencies began buying computers as well, both to speed up their work and to have a high-tech status symbol.

By the early 1950s computers had progressed beyond their military roots, establishing a toehold in the business world. IBM and other office-machine manufacturers started competing with UNIVAC, developing and selling their own lines of computers. This step made good financial sense: there are far more corporations than national governments, and it is easier to get a contract with a private firm than it is to do business with a public agency. Also, it was clear even in those early days of the computer age that these "robot brains" would replace many, if not all, of the mechanical office machines then in use. Any office machine manufacturer that did not have a business computer line to offer its customers was not likely to survive.

The first commercial computers were designed to do what punch-card tabulators had done for decades: speed up the process of office mathematics. Computers speeded up corporate accounting, from sending out monthly bills to calculating employee paychecks. They helped make it easier for insurance companies to determine rate tables, just as hand-operated calculators had done before. As the technology improved, people began developing business computers that could handle other, more complicated tasks. For example, the Semi-Automatic Business-Related Environment, or SABRE, system developed by IBM for American Airlines linked 1,200 Teletype terminals across the nation to a central reservation computer in New York. Travel agents and ticket counter clerks could instantly determine if seats were available for a given flight and book a passenger on that plane. (Until SABRE came on line in the early 1960s, after 10 years of development, airlines booked seats with the assistance of hundreds of employees who answered phones, updated wall-sized status boards, and tried not to put more than one person in the same seat at one time.)

IBM was the leader in the fledgling computer industry. Under the leadership of Thomas Watson Sr., IBM's president, the office-machine company had kept up with the latest trends in computer science. After constructing the Automatic Sequence Controlled Calculator for Harvard, IBM built another electromechanical computer, though this was more a way to demonstrate IBM's abilities than it was a serious push toward mechanical computers. When Eckert and Mauchly's UNIVAC I became the first commercial electronic computer to hit the market in 1950, Watson's engineers began designing vacuum-tube computers according to the Von Neumann architecture that had taken hold.

With its immense client base and its reputation for producing machines that worked well—particularly the punch card printers and readers that the new computers required—IBM was able to take an early lead in the commercial computing race. Other firms either hired engineers to set up computer divisions or purchased one of the small computer companies that had gone into business after World War II. For example, Remington Rand, one of IBM's rivals in the office-machine industry, took the second path when it purchased UNIVAC from Eckert and Mauchly in 1950. (Just in time, from UNIVAC's perspective. Though they were good engineers, the company's founders had been less than successful as businessmen—something that would happen many times in the computer world.)

"No More Than a Dozen"

There are so many computers in the world today that it is hard for people to comprehend how big a gamble it was for large firms like Remington Rand or IBM to get involved in building commercial computers. There was a market for the big calculators in the business world, but nobody knew exactly how big it would be—mainly because nobody knew how businesses would use these machines, which, after all, had been designed mainly as mathematic tools.

There is a legend in the computer world: In the early 1950s a reporter asked Thomas Watson Sr. how much demand there might be for the computers IBM was beginning to build. Supposedly, Watson said that computers eventually would be installed around the world—but no more than a dozen, since computers were such specialized machines that few governments or companies, and virtually no private citizens, would need to have one of their own. Others may not have shared this view, but in those days it was clear that computer makers were competing for a very limited number of customers who needed and could afford their products. And these companies competed fiercely for any contract, whether for a corporation's accounting computer or for a government data processing machine.

IBM took the lead in the computer industry, just as it had in the world of office machines. And even at a time when new computers were expected to be far superior to previous models, many of the company's contracts were highly impressive. In the 1950s, for example, IBM received a contract to build computers that had been created for one of the decade's biggest high-tech projects, the Semi-Automatic Ground Environment, or SAGE. SAGE was designed to help protect the continental United States from a bomber or missile attack during the cold war. (The acronym SAGE also was a play on words; a sage is a wise person who can calmly analyze and respond to situations.)

SAGE came into being at the Lincoln Laboratory, a computer research center that the Massachusetts Institute of Technology established in the early 1950s specifically to design and build the system. SAGE tied a network of radar stations into a series of computers that were programmed to identify potentially hostile aircraft. The computer—which by itself was called Whirlwind—also helped military personnel guide fighter-interceptor airplanes toward these targets to see if they were truly threats or not. The SAGE's Whirlwind computers displayed information using very simple dots and line drawings on circular video screens, along with letter-and-number, or alphanumeric, codes to identify these dots as friendly craft or as intruders.

Whirlwind's display was primitive compared to the displays available on today's computers, but it marked a major advance in the development of computing technology. The computer generated and displayed these images in what came to be called *real time*—in other words, the computer displayed the information gathered by its radar stations as fast as it received the signals, with nearly no delay in processing time. It

The SAGE early-warning system's Whirlwind computer contained a number of important advances that influenced the growth of computer technology. [Courtesy the MITRE Corporation]

accomplished this feat thanks to the use of magnetic-core memory, which cut down the computer's processing time dramatically. There still were vacuum tubes in the Whirlwind's processing circuitry, but they were fast enough not to interfere with the speed of the display.

When IBM took over the job of building and installing SAGE's computers for 23 command stations across the nation, the company could say that it either designed or built the most advanced computers in the world. Whirlwind and SABRE were stupendous achievements for their computing power, for their presentation of real-time data, and (in the SAGE system) for their advanced display tools. Transistors and magnetic cores were being combined with other improved components and advances in computer design with seemingly miraculous gains in performance. For all their speed and power, though, these machines were not quite supercomputers. Whirlwind was a specialized machine that had been built for a specialized military use. And SABRE, which would pioneer the use of real-time computing in the business world, was still just a very fast business computer. Supercomputers would be built for a different purpose—to aid science.

PART 2

Transition to Supercomputers

SEYMOUR CRAY'S
REFRIGERATED COMPUTERS

Computers started out as general-purpose calculating machines, and they pretty much stayed that way throughout the 1950s as computer designers and computer users learned what these machines could be made to do. Aside from SAGE, SABRE, and a few other large projects, there was no need for specialized computers. They were number crunchers, plain and simple—big machines that handled big blocks of data, one batch of punch cards or punch tape at a time. The components that went into the machines basically were the same, and each computer's designers based their work on the Von Neumann architecture. There were a few differences in the way the circuits of a science computer were designed when compared to a business computer, but the biggest difference between the two was the way they were programmed.

Toward the end of the 1950s, though, it was becoming clear that the "general purpose computer" really was not all that general in purpose. There was a definite split in needs between business uses and scientific uses. Business computers require the ability to handle a great variety of tasks at one time, such as tracking inventory, processing orders, and calculating prices and taxes. To do this work, a business computer needs to store lots of data, perform calculations using values that often change, and track many types of data. Scientific computers, on the other hand, generally have less variety in the tasks they handle but are required to perform them very fast.

The Need for Speed

At first, computer developers focused equally on improving speed and computing power, with their machines judged by the difficulty of the tasks they could handle as much as by the speed at which they worked. Of course, each new model of computer was supposed to be more powerful and faster than all the others, if only because each new model of computer generally was more expensive than all the others. Transistors made circuit boards smaller and faster, but there still were many other components on the boards. Though they were faster than their vacuum-tube predecessors, the second generation of computers was made up of a slow-operating group of machines.

The big obstacle to making faster computers was physics. It took time for electricity to flow through a computer's components and the wires that connected them. Electrons, the subatomic particles that make up electric currents, have the ability to travel at the speed of light—186,000 miles, or 299,793 kilometers, per second. In an ideal conductor, such as a *superconductor,* which shows no resistance to the flow of electricity, electricity travels about 1 foot per nanosecond. In wires, though, the actual speed is much slower, with the metal in the wire slowing down the electron flow, robbing energy, and radiating it away as heat. The same thing happens in the wire coils of a toaster or in the filaments of a light bulb.

Moreover, the length of the wires that connected the various sections of a computer slowed operating speeds even more. The processing units, memory units, and data storage units all were in separate cabinets, or, at best, separate sections of the same large cabinet. Control consoles were separate units connected to the central processor. A spiderweb of wiring shrouded the circuit boards within each of these cabinets, forcing electricity to travel through miles of metal as it worked its way through the circuits of the first- and second-generation computers. And the cables that connected the cabinets made the journey even longer.

All this wiring also increased the amount of power these computers consumed. Consider this image: 10 gallons of water flowing through a 10-foot-long garden hose will come out of the nozzle at a faster speed and with more pressure than the same amount of water flowing through a hose that is 20 feet long. The reason? Again, simple physics: flowing through the longer hose uses up more energy. With a long enough hose, the water would not even make it to the end. The same principal holds true with electricity—it takes more energy to send a current through a long wire than a short one, and more energy still to send current through hundreds of wires that have different lengths.

Pushing through all this electricity to keep the machine running created a lot of heat. Transistors did not burn out like vacuum tubes did, but the high temperatures could cause other failures throughout a computer system, such as melting the soldered connections that kept the circuits alive or frying the other components attached to the circuit boards. Up through the early 1960s, computers were air-cooled and, ideally, kept in air-conditioned rooms. This method usually worked; when it did not, the computers had to be shut off to protect their circuitry.

Computer designers faced functional and economic limits to getting rid of the heat problem. Computer components had to be packed close together so the computers would fit in as small a space as possible. Processors and memory units had to be easy to put together, use, and service. In addition, reliability was as important to customers as speed and computing power. Designers could not be too innovative in their attempt to introduce new components or new circuit designs. Customers would not want to buy computers that took too long to repair or broke down while a technological innovation was being tested.

Economically, computer designers were held back by the need to build machines that manufacturers could mass produce and that customers could afford. With any large-scale manufacturing process, it is more cost-effective to use parts that are good enough for a product's intended purpose than to use ones that are designed for a level of use they may never reach. A modern-day midsized car, for example, would be far more expensive if it was designed to race on the NASCAR circuit on a daily basis, rather than simply to run around town.

Even so, a few computer pioneers saw speed as a worthy goal to pursue.

Seymour Cray Enters the Fray

Seymour Cray was one of these pioneers. Born in 1925 in Chippewa Falls, Wisconsin, Cray served in the U.S. Army during World War II as a radio operator. As many veterans did, he went to college after the war was over, while working part time as a radio and TV repairman. He earned a bachelor's degree in electrical engineering in 1950 and a master's degree in applied engineering the following year, both from the University of Minnesota.

After finishing his college career, Cray went to work for Engineering Research Associates (ERA), a computer maker that a pair of former U.S. Navy engineers had opened in a former St. Paul, Minnesota, glider factory after World War II. The two men, William C. Norris and Howard Engstrom, had served in a code-breaking center in Washington, D.C., where they used a set of "bombes" like those at Bletchley Park in England to do their work. Norris in particular had a host of ideas for nonmilitary uses for the bombes, ranging from air traffic control systems to electronically controlled flight simulators. However, like most early computer makers, ERA spent its early years winning and working on government contracts.

Like its competitors, ERA wanted to make better computers. Unlike many other companies, though, ERA's management supported the work of mavericks, people who were willing to go against the accepted way of doing things and push the limits of their skills and their materials. This philosophy led to some interesting developments. In just a few years, for instance, the company was shopping around its computers to potential commercial users, touting a feature that was unique to ERA—a "magnetic drum memory." An early ancestor of the hard-disk drive, it was a metal cylinder with spark-plug-shaped magnetic heads that wrote information into an inner drum and read it off again.

ERA was the type of place that was ideal for someone like Cray, who had little tolerance for doing anything not directly related to making computers. He was able to put his skills to use without having to worry about following corporate procedures or sticking only to his assigned duties. He was interested in software, logic (the means by which computers handle instructions), and circuit design, and he soon became known for improving the design of machines he worked on—and even some that he had not been asked to improve. Before long, he was given the opportunity to design his first scientific computer, the ERA 1101.

In 1951, a little while after Cray started work at ERA, the company sold itself to Remington Rand, and Cray was asked to contribute to the design of non-ERA machines, including a UNIVAC model, the 1103. The machine was based on an older computer known as the ATLAS II, and Cray was asked to improve the computer's control system, a vital component that figured out the best way for a computer to act on its instructions. Cray was told to figure out a way to update and streamline the control system. He succeeded in a way no one expected him to: Instead of rebuilding the existing system, he created an entirely new one.

Cray went on to work on other machines at steadily increasing levels of responsibility, and, in some cases, created entirely new components as he went along. One of these was a magnetic switch that he created by wrapping a stainless-steel spool with a thin length of magnetic ribbon. It did the same job as a vacuum tube and the transistors developed by Bell Labs. In fact, it was such a good alternative to vacuum tubes that a team of former ERA engineers considered it as the main switching component when Remington Rand's UNIVAC Division bid on a project to build computers for the U.S. Air Force's Inter-Continental Ballistic Missile (ICBM) program in the mid-1950s.

In their St. Paul factory, the engineers, with Cray as their supervisor, evaluated his magnetic switches and some of the transistors then available to determine which would be better in the computer design they were drafting for the air force. Though the magnetic switches were reliable and were better understood than transistors, the team—Cray included—unanimously decided that transistors would be the better component both then and in the future. Ironically, another group of Rand engineers in Philadelphia—the original UNIVAC group led by J. Presper Eckert—won the contract using magnetic switches.

Even so, Cray was impressed with transistors and would turn to them a few years later as the centerpiece of the work that would consume the rest of his life. Having designed computers that the greatest number of potential users could buy, Cray decided that he wanted to build the fastest computers in the world, regardless of what the majority of computer customers wanted. He set upon a course that would turn away from the larger base of computer users and lead to a select group of customers: those who could afford to pay a few million dollars for a cutting-edge machine. In other words, Cray turned his back on the family-car market to build rocket cars.

As part of this new course, Seymour Cray left the UNIVAC factory in 1957. Shortly before he left, a group of longtime ERA veterans had formed a new company, Control Data Corporation (CDC), in a portion of a Minneapolis warehouse that was used to store rolls of newsprint for the two big newspapers in town. Cray joined up with his former colleagues and, to help CDC stay alive, began designing and building a new type of transistor-based computer.

Cray designed circuit boards that packed more components onto less space. He also, for a while, used factory-reject transistors that found their way to an electronics supply warehouse. The problem was that

Seymour Cray, seen here with the CRAY-2 supercomputer, not only created the first supercomputers but also started three companies to sell and improve his machines. [Courtesy Cray Inc.]

these transistors did not deliver consistent levels of performance. Some were lightning fast while others were very slow, and there was no way to determine if they were good or not without putting them in a circuit and testing them. Cray worked around this problem with a design that used two transistors in each processing module, which smoothed out the quality problems and yielded faster-than-normal operations.

This computer, which was named the CDC 1604, was Cray's first high-speed computer. It came out in 1960 with a clock speed of 0.2 megahertz. That level of performance meant that it could carry out an operation every five-millionths of a second, making it the fastest computer in the world (though it was not and is not considered a supercomputer). Before long, CDC was selling 1604s across the United States and around the globe: to the Naval Postgraduate School in Monterey, California; to aerospace giants Lockheed and Northrop;

and to the government of Israel, among others. The company also scored a major coup when the U.S. Atomic Energy Commission's Lawrence Livermore Laboratory bought one of the machines, a decision that was based on the 1604's programming manual and the positive experience of the National Bureau of Standards, which also had purchased one of the machines.

Keeping Computers Cool

The success of the 1604 meant that CDC had become a growing company, with all the paperwork, administrative tasks, and other chores that growing companies create. Unfortunately for CDC, Seymour Cray's main interest was to build the world's fastest computers, not to get involved in the world of business—or to listen to suggestions from cost-conscious project managers. He decided to leave the company, but allowed himself to be talked into staying in exchange for certain conditions. The main condition was that CDC would build a laboratory for Cray within walking distance of his home in Chippewa Falls, where he could work without interruptions from early in the morning until well into the night.

Cray, who always had been known for his long hours, became a recluse. He secluded himself from the rest of the world to concentrate on circuit diagrams. Rumor had it that Cray built his computers on a card table on the porch of his home, using tweezers and a soldering gun. (CDC helped support this rumor itself, since it made for good

The CDC 6600 was Seymour Cray's first supercomputer and the first acknowledged supercomputer in the world. The console of the room-filling computer featured two circular display screens. [Courtesy Lawrence Livermore National Laboratory and www.computer-history.info]

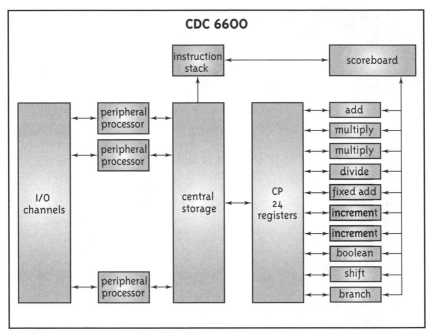

CDC 6600

This diagram of the CDC 6600 shows where Cray placed the various functions of the computer.

publicity and enforced the idea of its supercomputers as being unique machines.) But what Cray really used was a pencil and a pad of 8½-by-11-inch paper, on which he performed each day's calculations for his new computer design, the CDC 6600. Back at the CDC offices, the 30 or more people on his development team checked his figures, after which workers would assemble modules for the computer.

Cray had decided that the 6600 would be 50 times faster than the 1604, running with a clock cycle of 10 megahertz, or one ten-millionth of a second, rather than the 1604's 0.2 megahertz, or five-millionths of a second. This goal meant that the 6600's components had to be packed as tightly as possible, reducing the amount of space between components and cutting down the amount of wires running throughout the computers.

For all his innovation, though, Cray continued to be reluctant to use new technologies right away. Instead, he preferred to take proven components and push them to higher levels of performance. Integrated circuits, in which components were etched onto a circuit board rather than attached with solder, were available by the early

1960s, but Cray stayed with his transistor-based designs until well into the decade.

For the 6600, this reliance on transistors meant that an old problem would become even worse. Packing all those transistors—more than 350,000—as close together as they needed to be generated a huge amount of heat. It was clear that there would be far more heat than an air-cooling system could handle. Unless there was better way to cool the computer, it could not be switched on without having the machine cook itself to death.

Fortunately, there was a better way. Seymour Cray had M. Dean Rough, a mechanical engineer at CDC who once had designed commercial refrigerators and freezers, come up with something that had never been tried before: a refrigeration system mounted inside the computer. Rough studied the CDC 6600's design and figured out a way to install a Freon-based cooling unit in the available space within the computer's cabinets. Aluminum plates within the computer absorbed heat from the circuit boards and channeled it to a series of Freon-filled struts, which carried the heat away.

Supercomputers Hit the Market

The CDC 6600 was the first machine to be called a "supercomputer" by both its users and the news media. Nothing else was as fast as the 6600; nothing else could handle the tasks the 6600 could handle. CDC sold 63 of the supercharged computers for a minimum price of $7.5 million each (equivalent to roughly $43 million in 2002) from 1964 to 1967, with the first one going to the U.S. Atomic Energy Commission's Lawrence Livermore National Laboratory. That price was for the machine by itself; customers were expected to design the software they needed and to correct any problems (a six-month process with the first machine). The high price was justified by the unique nature of the machine, and by the fact that no one else was building comparable ones.

Cray designed two other CDC supercomputers, the CDC 7600 and the CDC 8600 (which was never built), but he eventually left CDC and started his own firm, Cray Research. The reason for Cray's departure was the same as for his earlier split from ERA. As a company matures, its managing officers and higher-ranking employees lose their desire to take risks and start focusing on maintaining a reliable, sustained level of growth. This shift was taking place at CDC at the beginning of the 1970s, as the company changed its focus from high-speed scientific supercomputers to commercial computers. Also, part of Cray's method of working was to start from scratch with each new computer design, without worrying about compatibility with previous models. This way of doing things was at odds with the common idea of customer service, which demanded that a new computer model should be able to work with its predecessors. Once again, Cray was willing to turn away from standard ways of doing business in order to pursue his dreams.

Cray Research, which Seymour Cray founded in 1972, was devoted solely to building supercomputers. Firmly set up in his new company, Cray designed yet another revolutionary computer, the CRAY-1. It was a revolution not just in computing power, but in Cray's own design methods. Cray finally shifted from soldered circuit boards to integrated circuits, using more than 200,000 chips in the computer, as well as 60 miles of wiring and 3,400 integrated circuit boards. It was much faster than any other machine that Cray, or anyone else, had ever built.

The CRAY-1 was the first supercomputer that was able to work on more than one part of a problem at a time. By using a technique called *vector processing*, the computer was able to carry out a single operation—such as multiplication—on a whole list of numbers simultaneously. And CRAY-1 was a revolution in the way computers looked. It was C-shaped when seen from the top, with a six-foot-high central tower and a partial ring of padded seats that formed its eight-foot-diameter base. The seats concealed the components that did not fit into the tower, including a refrigeration unit, and provided a place for technicians to sit. This design had a great practical effect: It allowed Seymour Cray to limit the length of the wires connecting the components inside the computer to a maximum of four feet, increasing the speed of operation.

The CRAY-1 went to work in the spring of 1976 at Los Alamos National Laboratory in New Mexico. Because of its computing capabilities and its appearance, many people considered the CRAY-1, rather than the CDC 6600, to be the world's first true supercomputer, though most historical accounts point to the CDC machine as the first of its class. Whatever the case, CRAY-1's debut marked the first real challenge in the decade-old market for high-speed computers.

For a good long while, CDC had a lock on the supercomputer market, even after it began shifting its focus to commercial machines. Other manufacturers, particularly IBM, tried to bring out their own

The CRAY-1 supercomputer, built by Cray Research in the early 1970s, continued the practice of using a built-in cooling system to maintain the computer's internal operating temperature. [Courtesy Lawrence Livermore National Laboratory]

high-speed computer systems, but they all had failed. Now the super-computer industry, and competition within the industry, was split between CDC and Cray Research. IBM, Honeywell, and other companies focused on building standard mainframe computers and exploring other forms of high-tech computing, such as the networked computer systems that eventually would form parts of the Internet. However, this state of business would not last.

RAISING THE STANDARDS

The invention of transistors had been a revolutionary advance in the building of computers, but it had not solved all the drawbacks of circuit design. Transistors still needed to be wired by hand onto circuit boards, the wires that connected them were large and cumbersome in comparison to the tiny components, and the connections sometimes failed. Also, in October 1957 the Soviet Union had put *Sputnik*, the world's first artificial satellite, into orbit. The following month, *Sputnik II* carried the first living animal into orbit, and a few years later the communist superpower launched a space capsule carrying Yuri Gagarin, the first human to orbit the planet. These events had sparked a space race between the Soviets and the United States, which was determined to beat the Soviets in this battle of technological superiority. In order to meet this goal, the nation needed faster and lighter-weight computers than transistors could provide.

Likewise, it took a few years before integrated circuits, or ICs, became the technological marvels they are today. Jack Kilby, an engineer at Texas Instruments—one of the world's most famous high-technology companies—developed the first IC in 1958, devising a way to build miniature transistors on a single silicon chip. Like other engineers who were developing new types of transistors, Kilby chose silicon as the semiconductor base of the circuit because it was cheaper than germanium or other materials, even though it was not as efficient a semiconductor. At first, the transistors were about the size of a match head, but they were small enough to make a compact electrical circuit that, in turn, could be placed on a larger circuit board.

Robert Noyce at Fairchild Semiconductor, another of the great computer technology firms, further shrank the size of computers. He created an integrated circuit whose transistors were connected by tiny metal lines printed on or imbedded in the silicon chip during the manufacturing process. This process of etching circuits in place on silicon chips not only made circuits smaller, it started a trend toward cramming more and more transistors onto silicon chips that was to last for decades. Even so, these first integrated circuits still needed to be wired together onto a larger circuit board.

By the time Cray used integrated circuits in his early-1970s supercomputers, ICs were a nearly 15-year-old technology. Improvements in techniques for etching microscopic transistors and wires onto silicon had led to the creation of microprocessors, circuit chips that incorporate computer control and processing elements that once took up refrigerator-sized cabinets. Once again, Seymour Cray had proven to himself the benefits of using new technologies after others had spent the time and money to fix their flaws and improve their good points.

By using integrated circuits in the CRAY-1, Seymour Cray was acknowledging not just the advantages that integrated circuits had over transistors but the speed at which the computer industry was evolving. In the 25 years after Cray started working for Engineering Research Associates, computers had exploded in speed and ability. The rate at which computer power increased boiled down to Moore's law, a rule of thumb in computer science first voiced by Gordon Moore, a cofounder of computer chip maker Intel Corp., during the 1960s. Moore noticed that computers double in power about every two years. That is, each new generation of computers works twice as fast, can handle twice as many functions at one time, and in general are twice as good as those available two years before. When Seymour Cray left CDC to start his own business, new techniques of designing and assembling circuits had yielded regular computers the size of a large cardboard box that contained more processing ability than the room-sized machines of the early 1950s.

By the 1970s it was clear that integrated circuits not only were going to be the heart of the next generation of computers but also were going to lead to generations of computers that would be smaller and more powerful than their predecessors. For supercomputer designers, though, Moore's law had its downside. As computer technology improved, the speed and power of past supercomputers gradually became less amazing. Less-costly computers started attaining levels of performance that equaled or were better than multimillion-dollar computers of a decade ago or less. Also, more companies began moving into the supercomputer field, giving both Cray Research and CDC their first real competition.

Competition in a High-Speed Race

At first, the supercomputer market was very tight. CDC and Cray Research were the only two companies that built supercomputers as their main product line, and of the two, Seymour Cray's firm was the better known. Not only had the CRAY-1 earned instant fame with its appearance and abilities, but Cray himself had become a technology celebrity during his years at CDC. In contrast, a few other computer firms tried to create their own line of supercomputers during the 1960s, when Seymour Cray was working for CDC, only to find that supercomputing was beyond their abilities.

IBM was one of the firms that tried to challenge Cray's dominance of high-speed computing. In the early 1960s the company decided to attack CDC's lock on the supercomputer market with the IBM 360/90, an advanced version of its popular 360 line of commercial computers that would be faster than the CDC 6600. IBM was counting on its overall fame in the business computer field to attract customers for the Model 90, as the machine became known.

Part of the drive to build the Model 90 and challenge CDC for customers stemmed from corporate pride. Albert Williams, who took over from Thomas Watson Sr. as president of IBM, felt that his internationally known firm should not allow the Minnesota company—which grew from 11 employees in 1957 to 9,000 in 1965 and was the number-three computer company behind IBM and the UNIVAC Division of Sperry-Rand (a company formed when Remington-Rand merged with a company called Sperry Gyroscope)—to dominate any area of the computer field. Also, the CDC machine was far from perfect. It needed extensive maintenance after every eight to nine hours of computation time, and despite the refrigeration system, its temperature could rise to dangerous levels—as high as 170 degrees Fahrenheit. These problems were not fixed until 1965, giving IBM's salesforce two big selling points for the Model 90.

At first, IBM's entry into the supercomputer field attracted a lot of interest from potential customers. Los Alamos National Laboratory signed up to take delivery of the first of these new supercomputers, while other IBM salesmen pursued contracts for commercial versions of the computer. However, IBM engineers ran into trouble turning the company president's directive into a working machine. Not only were they trying to solve problems that Seymour Cray had overcome years before, but they were trying to create a better machine than the CDC 6600 from scratch. Model 90 turned out to be a costly venture, one with numerous problems that made the machine less stable than the 6600. Aside from the Los Alamos laboratory and eight other customers, no one else was willing to buy the Model 90. In the end, IBM canceled the program, on which it had spent $126 million (roughly $710 million in 2003 dollars).

For the rest of the 1960s and the first half of the 1970s, no other company posed a serious challenge to CDC, aside from Seymour Cray's own company. There were a handful of other supercomputer makers: Texas Instruments, Burroughs, Sperry-Rand's UNIVAC Division, and even IBM, which made slower-speed computers than those of CDC and Cray Research. But supercomputers were only a sideline business for these companies, one that gave them a bit of extra business and prestige, as well as a research and development division that could pay for itself.

Part of this lack of competition came from a lack of need for supercomputing. The type of scientific and engineering research projects that required the speed and power of a supercomputer were limited, even in the early 1970s. Computers in general were still a bit of a novelty in those days before the personal-computer revolution, and expensive novelties at that; it was rare to see one outside a large college campus or a major corporation. Few customers could afford a supercomputer, and many of them were government agencies or military-supported research groups that needed the high-speed machines to perform the math-intensive calculations of nuclear weapons simulations.

As the 1970s progressed, though, supercomputers started to become necessary tools for analysis and simulation of phenomena in other fields of research. For example, the cold war had created a particularly deadly game of undersea cat-and-mouse between surface ships and attack submarines on one hand and "boomers," submarines that carried nuclear missiles, on the other. All three types of vessels used sonar to find where their opponents were in the three-dimensional playing field of the ocean and to pursue or escape from them. As submarines grew more quiet, though, it was harder to pick out their signals from the background noise of the ocean. Computers on board the vessels could help separate normal ocean sounds from human-made noise, but only if they contained a database of each type of sound. Supercomputers created these databases by analyzing sonar recordings and identifying the natural from the artificial.

There were a great many nonmilitary uses for supercomputers as well. Automobile designers and building engineers began using supercomputers to calculate the stresses and analyze the construction needs of their projects. Astronomers saw supercomputers as a way to test their theories of star formation and composition, as well as to explore possible explanations for the evolution of the solar system. Geologists ran the numbers from their analyses, including *seismic surveys*, of rock formations and other underground features tests on supercomputers in the search for deposits of oil or other resources.

The high cost of supercomputers gradually became less of an obstacle, as governmental organizations and corporate benefactors established supercomputer centers and sponsored supercomputer research at leading universities. Promoting the development and use of supercomputers, and helping scientists and other researchers gain easier access to the computational power of supercomputers, had two positive influences. They prevented a technology gap between advanced nations, and they served a public good by helping scientists advance their fields of study. Also, researchers who were unfamiliar with supercomputing could try out different models of supercomputers.

Because of this expanded use and interest in supercomputers, a new wave of companies began to challenge Cray Research and CDC. Some of these challengers were the well-known names in the computer world that had kept a toe in the supercomputer ocean. Others were relative newcomers. For example, by the mid-1980s, Cray Research and CDC had three competitors from Japan: Fujitsu, Hitachi, and NEC, all of which had governmental support from Japan's Ministry of International Trade and Industry, which helped Japanese corporations compete in the international market.

Later on, challengers to supercomputer sales and opportunities to exploit supercomputer technology came from new areas. The personal-computer boom of the 1980s, which stemmed from the 1970s invention of the *minicomputer* and the development of such machines as the Apple, also sparked a number of companies that later became supercomputer powerhouses. One of these, Silicon Graphics, Inc. (SGI), got its start in 1983 by building graphics *workstations* that had as much power as a mainframe computer in a system a little larger than a modern tower-sized personal computer. Within a few years, it became one of the leading manufacturers of graphics-specific computers that were used for *computer-aided design*, three-dimensional computer animation, and *virtual reality*. Because its machines already incorporated a lot of power in a small package, SGI naturally went into the supercomputer business and made some of the top-rated machines in the world. Compaq Computer Corp. took a similar path. It started in 1983 as a personal-computer (PC) maker that focused on making machines for small and medium-sized businesses. It gradually increased its product line to include larger systems, with central mainframe computers and PC-style terminals, and was making supercomputers by the mid-to-late 1990s. (It merged with Hewlett-Packard in 2001.)

By 1993 there were enough supercomputers and manufacturers in the world for realistic comparisons between systems. Computer scientists at the University of Tennessee and the University of Mannheim in Germany, established a "top 500" ranking system of the 500 most powerful computers in the world based on how fast they could complete a set of benchmark calculations. The test was designed to rank computers based on their real-world performance, as opposed to each manufacturer's estimate maximum number of operations.

Twenty-five Years of Supercomputer Growth

From 1975 to the end of the 20th century, supercomputer technology took a fairly straight path leading from the CRAY-1 to the Top 500 list.

Cray Research's next supercomputer was the CRAY-2, which Seymour Cray began designing around the time the CRAY-1 went to work at the Los Alamos National Laboratory. Cray wanted his company's third computer (the second was the CRAY-1S, a slightly more powerful version of CRAY-1) to be four to six times more powerful than its predecessors. Like CRAY-1, the CRAY-2 was housed in a C-shaped cabinet, this one packed with 240,000 computer chips. However, Cray decided that the longest wire in the CRAY-2 had to be no longer than 16 inches, rather than the 48 inches of the longest CRAY-1 wire, to get the performance he wanted. That constraint meant packing the supercomputer's components into a far smaller space, one measuring only 53 inches across and 45 inches tall.

Designing a supercomputer that could fit into this space took years; in fact, the first CRAY-2 did not go to work until 1985. However, when it did leave company's assembly floor, the CRAY-2 had the largest internal memory of the time, with a capacity of 2 million bytes or 256 million words' worth of central memory, compared to the CRAY-1's 1 million. Its components included four processors that were linked together to yield a four-nanosecond clock speed, allowing it to process 1.2 billion floating-point operations, or flops, per second—up to 12 times faster than the CRAY-1.

Packing all this performance into a C-shaped cabinet that was less than four feet tall and 14 feet around—not counting the gap in the open side of the "C"—had created a big problem. Even the innovative refrigeration methods Cray had used for more than a decade, starting with the CDC 6600, would not cool the computer enough to keep it from burning out. The components would be too tightly packed and would generate too much heat, so much so that Cray and his engineers had to devise a unique way to keep the CRAY-2 running.

With its visible cooling system bubbling away, the CRAY-2 supercomputer was visually appealing as well as computationally powerful. [Courtesy Cray Inc.]

This was such a difficult question to answer that it took until 1981 for them to find a solution. Cray learned of a liquid coolant called Flourinet that 3M—one of the world's leading chemical and mining companies—had developed as a way to help patients survive heart surgery. Surgeons cannot operate on a person's heart unless they stop the heart and send the patient's blood through a machine that takes over the function of the heart and the lungs. Stopping the heart safely, though, involves cooling it—as with other muscles, the colder the heart is, the more slowly it works. Flourinet was designed to remove heat quickly without chemically interacting with the tissues of a patient's body.

Cray figured that this chemically inert coolant was just the solution he needed for the CRAY-2. Rather than using metal plates to absorb heat and carry it to cooling tubes, CRAY-2 would have its circuit boards sitting directly in a stream of Flourinet that would flow through the inner workings of the supercomputer. This idea was utterly revolutionary. Common sense said that bathing electronics in any type of liquid, inert or not, would short-circuit a computer. However, a test model of the design proved both that the cooling method was safe and that it was highly efficient. It also was beautiful: As the coolant flowed over the components and absorbed their heat, it began to boil, creating a string of bubbles that were carried away by the stream. When CRAY-2 became operational, its housing included a large window and an internal light that showed this effect, prompting one scientist to refer to it as "a computer in an aquarium."

Once again, Seymour Cray found himself in a growing company, and once again, he did not like it. He once said of himself, "I do tend to look forward in my thinking, and I don't like to rest on my laurels." In the early 1980s Cray gave up day-to-day control of his company and began to serve as an independent contractor, designing and building computers for the company that carried his name.

Cray kept on designing ever-faster and more powerful supercomputers. In 1984 he started on his next design, the CRAY-3, which had 16 processors and an 8-billion-byte memory. It also had a new type of computer chip, one made with gallium arsenide as its semiconductor base rather than silicon. Gallium arsenide chips had been invented recently and had proven themselves to be six to 10 times faster than their silicon counterparts. However, gallium arsenide is far more brittle than silicon, and computer chips made with gallium arsenide are more difficult to manufacture. To ensure that the chips were consistently reliable, Cray convinced Cray Research to open its own chipmaking facility.

Meanwhile, in April 1982, Cray Research announced a new series of computer systems, the CRAY X-MP. These were the first CRAY computers that Seymour Cray did not design. Instead, the X-MP's chief designer was Steve Chen, a Chinese immigrant who had worked on the CRAY-1 computers. The CRAY X-MP was 10 times faster than the original CRAY-1 and could perform 1 billion flops, or one gigaflop, twice as fast as any of those built by Japanese computer makers, which were challenging the American manufacturers. The X-MP was about the same size and shape as the CRAY-1, and it had two extra tower-and-bench modules: an input/output subsystem, and a solid-state storage device.

During this time, the definition of what made supercomputers "super" was changing dramatically. In 1976 a CRAY-1 performed more than 80 megaflops, or million operations per second. The CRAY X-MP4's gigaflop performance came in 1989. In 1991 the number-one supercomputer in the top 500 performed at 124.5 gigaflops. By com-

The CRAY X-MP/4, which offered 10 times the performance of the CRAY-1, was the first Cray Research supercomputer that was not designed by Seymour Cray.
[Courtesy Cray Inc.]

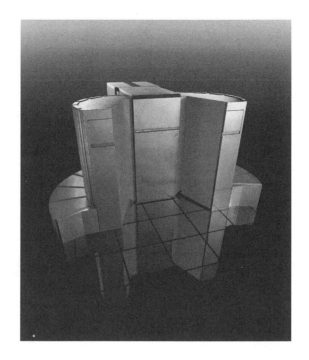

The CRAY X-MP/8 continued to improve upon the performance of previous supercomputers. [Courtesy Cray Inc.]

parison, the top-ranked supercomputer in the summer of 2002 was the Earth Simulator at Japan's Earth Simulator Center, which ran at a speed of nearly 36 teraflops, or trillion floating-point operations per second.

At the same time, the idea of how to get to the "super" level also changed. In the last decade of the 20th century, computer scientists found ways to get around the high cost of supercomputers by turning away from the standard pattern of loading large boxes with densely packed microprocessors.

9

PUTTING THE "SUPER" IN SUPERCOMPUTERS

While Seymour Cray was blazing the trail of high-speed computing, others followed a path that led to less-advanced but more-widely-used computers. With advances in transistors and integrated circuits during the 1960s and 1970s, computers gradually shrank. Minicomputers that could fit inside a single packing crate appeared in the mid-1960s, and *microcomputers*, which launched the era of the personal computer (PC), appeared in the 1970s.

These days, PCs have the same overall design, and it is easy to describe a typical computer system. Most PCs have a single motherboard that holds a single *central processing unit,* or CPU, the microprocessor whose circuitry performs the main calculation work. Various other chips—wired directly to the motherboard or to separate circuit boards that attach to it—form the computer's memory, generate sounds, plot images, and handle other tasks. Wire cables, infrared sensors or short-range radio signals connect PCs to accessories such as video monitors, keyboards, printers, or mice.

There are some variations to this pattern, such as "notebook" computers that combine most of the PC's elements in a single, portable case; hand-held computers such as personal digital assistants, or PDAs;

or desktop computers that combine all their components in one or two units. And PCs can be linked together through Ethernet connections, much as a radio receiver and a tape recorder can be wired together. In general, though, these variations are limited, and most PCs have similar designs and components. The same applies to larger computer systems, such as those that link computer terminals to a CPU or connect personal computers to each other and a central *server.*

For the first few decades of the supercomputer era, it was easy to point to a typical example of the new high-speed computing technology. At first, the only supercomputers were the ones built by Seymour Cray for CDC and, later, for Cray Research. Each company's machines were easy to identify, even though each new model was different from the last (since Seymour Cray believed in starting each new design from scratch). Then more companies entered the field, bringing in other designers who had differing ideas of how best to build a supercomputer.

Because of all these different approaches to supercomputer design, there is no such thing as a typical supercomputer. Each one is unique, especially the largest supercomputers that handle such immense tasks as calculating models of the world's climate or running simulations of supernovas. In a sense, all supercomputers are custom-made and hand-fitted: each one has to be configured for the tasks its users want it to perform, and it has to be installed by teams of workers that unload the machines from as many as a couple of dozen delivery trucks.

Even so, supercomputers share similar features that separate them from other computing systems.

Inside a Modern Supercomputer

One of the elements that supercomputers have in common is a CPU. Just as a personal computer does, supercomputers need a component that keeps track of tasks that are being completed, of data from tasks that have been finished, and of tasks that are yet to be done. For supercomputers, though, a CPU is a computer in its own right, one that even by itself could be a full-scale supercomputer. For example, the CPU at the San Diego Supercomputer Center (SDSC)—one of the first five supercomputing centers to be sponsored by the National Science Foundation in 1985—originally was a CRAY X-MP/48, which had an 8.5-nanosecond clock speed and was by itself one of the fastest supercomputers of its day. Its job was to coordinate the activity of a number of supercomputers and additional components that had been linked to yield an even higher level of performance.

In order to speed up their computing tasks, to handle the long and difficult programs they must run, supercomputers need large "active memories." Supercomputers must store massive amounts of data to be worked on, as well as intermediate results for the computations that are under way, and then be able to pick them up again when needed. In a supercomputer with more than one high-speed microprocessor, each processor may have its own memory; all the processors may, in addition, share a central memory. Some supercomputer manufacturers build their machines with a solid-state storage device (SSD), a collection of many computer chips linked to the supercomputer's CPU.

In addition, a supercomputer has to have a place to store information that may be needed in the future rather than in the next few hundred nanoseconds. For long-term data storage, supercomputers, like personal computers, write information either to hard-disk drives, high-capacity removable disks, or tape cartridges that resemble videotape cassettes.

The amount of memory and data storage space that supercomputers need is a way to gauge how fast computer technology has advanced. In the early 1990s, one supercomputer at the SDSC used a high-capacity, and high-cost, memory system that held an astounding (for the time) 15 gigabytes of data on a series of hard disks. Another supercomputer, an IBM 4381, had 50 gigabytes of on-line disk memory. And even with this enormous storage capacity, users had to move the information from the disks to another storage device within 36 hours or risk having it erased automatically to avoid cluttering the storage system. By contrast, a modern personal computer is considered less than adequate if its hard-disk drive has less than 40 gigabytes of storage space, and higher-capacity drives can be purchased for just a few hundred dollars.

Getting information into and out of the system is another area of supercomputer similarity. Because of the high volume of data and the high speed of operation, supercomputers need other computers to oversee the *input* and *output* of information. In any computer, input is the data or information that a user enters, while output is the information the computer gives back. Programs that control communication between a computer's components while they are turning input into output use *protocols*, or specific communications standards, that ensure each part understands the information that another part is sending. The same process applies to communication between the different parts of a supercomputer, with two important distinctions. The communication protocols within a supercomputer have to be written tightly enough to make full use of the computer's abilities, without clogging it up with unneeded instructions. And in order for the many parts of a supercomputer to work together properly, they must be properly linked.

The main information carrier in a supercomputer is called a *hyperchannel*, which gets its name from the huge amount of data it can carry. Essentially, a hyperchannel is like a huge dedicated phone line or a fiber optic cable, such as those that provide high-speed Internet access. In many ways, in fact, the input, output, and communication processes in a supercomputer are similar to those of the Internet, which links hundreds of millions of computers all over the world. The many different types of computer on the Internet "talk" to each other through a coding language called Transmission Control Protocol/Internet Protocol (TCP/IP). Supercomputers use similar protocols in rapidly transferring signals through its circuitry.

None of these improvements over standard computing technology make supercomputers "super" by themselves. Instead, it is the arrangement of a supercomputer's components and the way it handles the programs its users give it to run, as much as the number of components that are packed into its cabinets, that make supercomputers so much faster than other machines.

The Importance of Parallel Processing

Until the 1970s most computers were built following Von Neumann architecture, the description of EDVAC's inner workings that the mathematician wrote in the middle of the 1940s. As he described it—and as its inventors, John Mauchly and J. Presper Eckert, designed it—EDVAC used one central processor to perform all the operations needed to solve a calculation. The processor performed each of the operations one after the other, or serially, in a sequence of single steps. The computer spent much of its time sending data back and forth between its processor and its memory circuits, pulling out data and instructions for how to use it, and storing the results until its task was done.

However, this design has its drawbacks, particularly where speed is a concern. The only ways to make a Von Neumann computer faster are to make its circuits faster or to build it with preprocessors, circuits that take over some operations from the central processor. Simply having faster circuits is not enough to handle the huge amount of work that modern supercomputers perform. This was not true in the past. When computers were being developed, the rapid increase in their speed of operation was enough to satisfy most of the calculation needs of their day. Replacing the mechanical gears of Vannevar Bush's differential analyzer and the electromechanical relays of the Automatic Sequence Controlled Calculator with ENIAC's and EDSAC's electronic vacuum tubes was hailed as a remarkable advance. Then transistors produced a breakthrough that lowered costs, increased reliability, and sped up operations immensely. The invention of the integrated circuit and the very large-scale integrated microchip started the era of nanosecond computer operations.

However, only so many transistors and circuits can be squeezed onto a single silicon chip. This fact of physics is similar to that which Seymour Cray came up against when he built his last transistor-based supercomputers, and realized that he had reached the limits of how far he could shrink the distance between transistors without adopting integrated circuits. To work around the limitations of silicon chip technology, Cray and the supercomputer designers who followed him used multiple microprocessors, assisted by many more preprocessors, memory chips, and other components.

Increasing the speed of computer operation by using several processors, each working on one part of a problem simultaneously with the others, has been compared to the switch from a single-piston internal combustion engine to one that has four or more cylinders. Using several processors at one time turned out to be an ideal way to run extremely complex programs, and interest in using that method to achieve faster computing blossomed when the CRAY-2, which had up to four processors, reached the supercomputer market.

Some supercomputers use only a few full-scaled processing units; these machines are called *coarse-grained systems.* Supercomputers that use large numbers of less-powerful processors are called *fine-grained systems.* Some fine-grained systems have thousands of processors, each of which processes as few as one bit (one-eighth of a byte) of information at a time.

However, the number of processing units alone does not determine a supercomputer's overall speed. Tests done at Lawrence Livermore National Laboratory showed that a computer with four processors was only about 3.7 times faster than a single-processor machine. One reason that the four-processor computer was not four times faster was that the larger computer had to spend more time coordinating the information being sent from one group of components to another. Part of the time, a processor was communicating with the other three, rather than performing the calculations needed to solve part of the problem. At other times, there was a pause between the time when one or more of the processors completed a set of calculations and the time they were able to get data for the next set.

In order to wring as much performance out of the processors as possible, supercomputer designers have to choose the best method for dividing the tasks among them. Vector processing, the method Seymour Cray used, uses all the processors to carry out a single operation on an entire list of numbers at once. This was the best method for the first Cray Research supercomputer, which only had a single central processor but a huge amount of active memory. With multiple processors, however, the way was open for a different approach.

Parallel processing is a method of carrying out several operations, or several parts of a large operation, on a computer at the same time. To perform this large amount of work, a computer's internal architecture (the arrangement of its component parts) is set up to divide various parts of a single operation, or to distribute a number of separate operations, among more than one CPU, storing the results and combining them into a single answer when all portions of the task are finished. This method has become the more popular of the two with American supercomputer designers, though some vector processing systems have scored highly in measurements of supercomputer performance.

Parallel processing systems have a distinguished history; in fact, they have been around for millions of years. Brains, especially the human brain, are extremely efficient parallel processing systems. Communication among the parts of the brain is so quick and efficient that it is difficult to imagine duplicating the brain's power with an electronic device or machine. However, computer designers have tried to emulate the brain's function with high-speed switching systems, though none have come close to the speed and abilities of the real thing.

Supercomputer designers create parallel-processing machines using a few different methods. One method, called *pipelining*, resembles the sequence of operations in an assembly line. Several operations—such as getting data ready to work on, calculating sums, and storing the results from previous operations—take place at the same time as the data flows through the system. Much the same thing happens on an automobile assembly line, with workers performing different tasks as the entire car proceeds from station to station. The term *pipelining* comes from the way that the sequence of operations flows like water through a pipeline, with each operation starting as soon as the previous one is completed.

Another parallel-processing technique is called *functional parallelism*. This method is like building a car using several assembly lines, with workers on one assembly line assembling the body and chassis of the car, those on another line building engines, and a third group putting together the car's interior. Each of these parts would not be combined until they reached the end of their assembly lines. Likewise, functional parallelism allows separate parts of the supercomputer to work on small parts of a job; each result is then combined with the rest of the data to reach a final answer.

With another technique, *data parallelism*, the computer performs the same operation on separate portions of a problem's data. This is like setting up an assembly line to build all the engines of a day's run of cars, then all the suspension systems, then all the interiors, with final assembly taking place only after each portion is finished. With this method, the speed at which the supercomputer operates is determined by the amount of data it works with, not by the number of steps in its overall task. The important distinction between data parallelism and other methods is that the data drives the speed of the task. The more data there is, the faster a data-parallelism computer can complete the task, as compared to other machines. This means that a computer with this type of parallel architecture may be able to process two or three times as much data in the same length of time by adding extra processors to the job.

There have been problems with parallel processing, one of which is that *operating programs* generally have not been standardized to be used both with parallel or classic Von Neumann serial systems. There have been exceptions, of course. One of these, Occam, was developed in 1983 at Oxford University in England and was used by a number of supercomputer programmers and researchers. And since the early 1990s, various supercomputer makers have been adopting versions of a well-known programming language called UNIX, which was developed by AT&T Bell Laboratories in 1971 as an "open-source" language that could be adjusted for use on any computer system.

Also, while parallel processing has been the method of preference in the United States, the most powerful American-built system, the IBM-built ASCI White at Lawrence Livermore National Laboratory, was beaten by a Japanese-built vector-processing supercomputer in a 2002 study of supercomputer processing speed.

Shrinking Boxes to Fit the Components

Just as there is no typical supercomputer system, there is no typical supercomputer shape. The distinctive shape of the CRAY-1 and CRAY-2 machines captured the public's attention in the 1970s, and many of the supercomputers in the 1980s and early 1990s were touted as much for their small size as for their computational power. The CM-2 Connection Machine by Thinking Machines, a supercomputer manufacturer of the 1980s and early 1990s, was promoted with a picture showing its curved, waist-high control console in front of a slightly taller, cube-shaped cabinet built to look like a modern sculpture of eight smaller cubes packed next to and on top of each other.

In contrast, most of today's supercomputers are similar to the room-filling vacuum-tube machines of the 1950s, with rows of locker-sized cabinets sitting in well-cooled rooms within a computing center. Of course, these computers are capable of performing tasks that would have been unthinkable in the days of the second-generation and even the early third-generation computers. As with all other forms of electronics, modern supercomputers can pack more computing power into a smaller space than was possible even five years ago. For example, one of the most powerful supercomputers in the early 21st century, the IBM ASCI White at Lawrence Livermore National Laboratory, took up more than 9,900 square feet of floor space with its 106 tons of microprocessors, memory, and other components, with which it performed 7 trillion mathematical operations each second. And the most powerful computer in early 2002, the $350-to-$400-million Earth Simulator supercomputer system at Japan's Earth Simulator Research and Development Center, was built inside a room the size of a small airplane hangar, with 5,120 CPUs contained inside 640 separate supercomputing nodes.

The huge amount of space these machines take up may seem like a step backward when compared to the tidy boxes that make up most personal-computer systems. However, consider this fact: today's new personal computers, with their multigigahertz processors, multigigabyte hard drives, compact-disk recorders, and hundreds of megabytes of memory, operate at levels that once were considered the sole realm of multimillion-dollar supercomputers. The fact that people have machines such as these in their homes shows how far supercomputers have come since their early days, and how hard supercomputer developers have worked to push their advanced designs even farther.

10

THE BUSINESS OF SUPERCOMPUTERS

Supercomputers are the ultimate level of special-purpose electronics. In contrast to the hundreds of millions of PCs, laptops, and similar computers in use around the world today, supercomputers rarely appear outside research centers and office buildings. The computer industry as a whole sells hundreds of billions of dollars' worth of computers and components every year. In 2000, however, supercomputer manufacturers sold an estimated $5.6 billion worth of supercomputing systems. The relatively small number of supercomputers comes partly from the low number of people who need immediate access to a supercomputer's enormous calculating abilities. As following chapters discuss, the power of supercomputing is suited only to tasks in which a library's worth of raw data needs to be turned into a usable form. Compared to the work that mainstream computers perform, there are not many of these tasks.

The limited number of supercomputers also is due to the cost of one of these machines and of keeping it running long enough to justify the expense. Because there is a small need for supercomputers, there is only room in the world for a small group of supercomputer manufacturers. To make a profit on these highly complex products, which can consume millions of dollars' worth of components and labor, companies that make supercomputers have to charge their customers even more millions of dollars for their products. While low-end supercomputers, such as graphics workstations and systems whose designs are a few years old, cost as little as $10,000—the most advanced, up-to-date supercomputers cost nearly $100 million.

In addition, supercomputers use huge amounts of energy—enough power in some cases to operate hundreds of regular PCs constantly for a year. Owning a supercomputer can mean spending millions of dollars a year just to keep the machine running, and even more money to pay for maintenance and repair. Few groups can afford this type of expense, aside from governments, huge corporations, and large universities with a lot of financial support. Fortunately, there are enough potential customers who *can* afford these expenses, and enough prestige to be had in making some of the highest of the world's high-tech products, to keep a handful of supercomputer makers in business.

Putting the Pieces Together

Buying a supercomputer is not like picking up a laptop from a local store or ordering a custom-made desktop PC over the phone. For one thing, setting up a supercomputer is a major project in itself. Many supercomputers take up more square feet of floor space than most people have in their homes, and it takes hours for a team of technicians to put one together. The first supercomputers based on integrated circuits, such as the CRAY-1 and its immediate successors, took up a sizeable patch of floor space on their own, even with just a few cabinets clustered together. Even the CRAY-3—which some people called "the breadbox computer" because it was only one-fifth the size of the CRAY-2—was the size of a large-screen television. And the days in which such small machines were sufficient for the most advanced supercomputing tasks are long gone.

For example, in the late 1990s the Lawrence Livermore National Laboratory needed to upgrade its computing capacity. The laboratory is a major facility for nuclear weapons research that the U.S. Department of Energy maintains, east of San Francisco, California. Groups such as this have been major consumers of computing power going back to the 1950s, when researchers jumped at the chance to have computers perform the tedious, time-consuming work of calculating atomic interactions. Because international law forbids nuclear weapons, Lawrence Livermore's researchers simulate and analyze nuclear detonations on computers. In the real world, these phenomena take place over fractions of a second, with reactions taking place in spaces as small as the width of two atoms. There is no such thing as a computer that is too powerful to assist scientists in this type of work.

After asking a number of supercomputer manufacturers to bid on the project, Lawrence Livermore awarded the contract to IBM, which agreed to build and install a version of its RS/6000 supercomputer, which contained 8,192 microprocessors that could perform above the 12-teraflop level—for roughly $100 million. IBM was not the first company to make nuclear simulation systems. Other companies had built similar, though less powerful, supercomputers for the Department of Energy. The most recent of these was a series of computers called ASCI Blue. "ASCI" stood for "Accelerated Strategic Computing Initiative," a Department of Energy program to increase the use and development of supercomputers as tools for nuclear weapons simulation. Each ASCI computer was identified with a separate, government-assigned color code. The government and IBM decided to stick with this naming pattern and called the new machine ASCI White.

ASCI White was destined to become the leading supercomputer in the world in 2000—but only after IBM packed it in a convoy of 12 full-size trucks and sent it on a cross-country journey to the laboratory in northern California. It then took the better part of two months to unload the boxes and crates that contained the machine, assemble the components, and ensure that ASCI White was ready to do its work. Teams of technicians spent hundreds of hours testing connections, tracking down malfunctions, and fixing the various problems that crop up whenever a machine of this size is assembled.

It took about three years from the time IBM began work on ASCI White to the day the computer was ready to go to work. When that day came, the new supercomputer was the fastest, most powerful computer in use anywhere on the planet. Yet, for all the effort it took to design and assemble ASCI White, the computer held its title for less than a year before Japan's Earth Simulator became the world's top supercomputer. Not that ASCI White could be considered obsolete—it still was one of the fastest supercomputers in the world, and it seemed likely to be so for years to come. However, ASCI White's rapid displacement from the top of the heap illustrates how quickly things change in the field of supercomputing. In the time that it takes one company to assemble its latest model of supercomputer, other companies are at work on designs for systems that are even faster and more powerful. The same thing happens with personal computers, portable electronics, cars, and even vacuum cleaners. With supercomputers, though, pushing the technological limits is much harder.

How to Design a New Machine

So, how does a supercomputer come into being in the first place?

Formerly, designing a supercomputer meant designing a completely new system from scratch, from microprocessors to circuit boards to specially shaped cabinets. Seymour Cray was the master of this art. His CRAY-3 supercomputer contained its 16 processors and 8-billion-byte memory in a three-foot-tall cabinet, thanks to two design innovations. The first was Cray's decision to use custom-designed gallium arsenide chips in place of slower, silicon-based processors. The other was the fact that the longest wire in the machine was three inches long, which drastically cut down the speed it took to send information between the computer's components.

Many supercomputer designers tried to emulate the innovative shapes of the CRAY-1, CRAY-2, and CRAY-3 computers. In the early 1980s Seymour Cray's successor in supercomputer design at Cray Research, Steve Chen, finished work on the CRAY X-MP, a machine designed to be the successor to the CRAY-2. X-MP had three towers, rather than the single-tower design of CRAY-1 and CRAY-2. In addition to the C-shaped processing tower with its cooling unit hidden beneath a padded bench, X-MP had two additional wedge-shaped towers: a separate input-output subsystem and a solid-state storage device. The supercomputer needed these extra components to reach the speed of 1 billion operations per second that Chen and others at the company wanted it to achieve. But the extra towers still had the same curved-seat design of the original CRAY-1, placing them firmly in the same family as the machines Seymour Cray had designed.

For a few years supercomputer designers were able to keep within the boundaries set by these small, dynamic machines. By the early 1990s, however, it was clear that the only way to make more powerful supercomputers was to make bigger supercomputers. The designers simply could not cram any more components onto a processing chip or fit any more circuit boards into a cabinet. Faster computers needed more components, and more components required more cabinet space. At the same time, many of the companies that made these powerful machines decided they could not keep making their own microproces-

Japan's Earth Simulator was the most advanced example of a top-of-the-line super-computer in 2002. Its thousands of microprocessors contained the power needed to model the planet's climate and perform other types of analysis. (Courtesy the Earth Simulator Center)

sors. It was expensive to make microchips, especially with exotic materials such as gallium arsenide, or to pay another company to make chips to supercomputer-level standards. Soon the cost of making supercomputers would be so high that companies would not be able to charge enough to make a profit.

Fortunately, supercomputer designers received a couple of breaks from the general computing industry. A particularly big help was the development of extremely powerful commercial microprocessors that were fast enough to be used in a supercomputer's circuitry. Well-known companies such as Intel and Advanced Micro Devices (AMD), whose CPUs formed the heart of desktop and laptop computers, began shipping components to supercomputer factories, where they were wired into vector, parallel, or other processing arrays. Though individually they were not as fast as custom-designed chips, the commercial-grade processors performed well when they were connected.

Another benefit that came from the commercial computing field was the commercial computing systems themselves. Companies such as IBM, Sun Microsystems, Compaq, and Hewlett-Packard entered the supercomputer arena by taking their most advanced computing systems and turning them into supercomputers. Usually, these conversions were a matter of adding extra processors and memory, though they also could include separate computing subsystems for coordinating the supercomputer's tasks or combining results of different computations.

Shortcuts such as these, as well as the knowledge gained from earlier supercomputers, helped designers create the machines that were put into use throughout the late 1990s and early 2000s. Rather than drawing up new supercomputers from scratch, designers these days seek to improve existing designs to yield the desired performance levels. There also is little resistance to adopting new techniques and components that might give a new system a processing edge—and a marketing edge—over its competitors.

On the other hand, some facets of supercomputer design have not changed since the days when Seymour Cray was seeking ways to pack circuit boards together in the CDC 6600. When drawing up the plans for new machines, supercomputer designers look for any way to reduce the travel time between components. This task is hard enough when connecting microprocessors within one of a supercomputer's many cabinets; it becomes even harder when connecting all these cabinets together into a single calculating powerhouse. One system, in fact, has a maximum cable length of one meter, or roughly three feet.

The Rise and Fall of Supercomputer Stars

In the 1990s a pair of computer scientists—one in Germany, the other in the United States—began ranking the top 500 supercomputers around the world, measuring them by how fast they performed a standardized set of calculations. As each of the twice-yearly rankings came out, it usually showed that a field of nine or 10 companies was building most of the world's fastest machines. Some of these companies, such as the ones Seymour Cray founded, were started specifically to make supercomputers. Others, such as IBM or Hewlett-Packard, began building supercomputers as an extension of their existing business. And, over time, some well-regarded companies dropped out of the rankings after going out of business or shifting their focus to other areas of computing while others entered. The supercomputer market has held steady, though, with a limited number of manufacturers selling a limited number of machines to a limited number of customers.

As with any other young industry, the supercomputer business was dominated by a small number of easily identified people as well as by a small group of companies in its early days. Seymour Cray, the creator of the scientific supercomputer, swiftly became the hero of the ongoing supercomputer story. The man who succeeded him as head designer at Cray Research, Steve Chen, also became a sort of supercomputer celebrity with the release of the X-MP. As more companies began building supercomputers, though, the machines' novelty and the unique status of their designers rapidly diminished. Also, the job of designing supercomputers swiftly became more than one person could handle, even with the type of support available at Cray Research. Design teams, rather than individual geniuses, began creating the latest high speed computers.

At the same time, a new wave of competition was approaching from overseas. Japan, which had one of the world's leading electronics industries, put its skills to use in the realm of high-speed computing. Some of Japan's leading computer manufacturers, including NEC and Hitachi, began developing supercomputers of their own and selling them abroad. This challenge to the American-born supercomputing industry sparked a transpacific rivalry that has continued into the 21st century, creating some dramatic changes over the years.

Cray Research, for instance, has gone through a number of shake-ups since the early 1990s. Silicon Graphics, Inc. (SGI), a company that made highly advanced computers for engineers, industrial designers, and computer-graphics artists, bought Cray in the early 1990s. Though SGI had been in business only since 1982, it had done well enough to expand into the realm that Cray Research helped build and decided that buying the older company would help its business. Toward the end of the 1990s, though, Silicon Graphics sold Cray Research to another computer manufacturer, which took Cray's name for itself. As a result, the Cray name still is a feature of the modern supercomputing world.

Sadly, the ranks of modern-day supercomputer designers do not include the man who created the field, nor does the modern supercomputer industry contain the company that produced the first of his mighty scientific machines. Seymour Cray died in a car crash in 1996, while he was in the process of starting up yet another supercomputer company. And Control Data Corporation, which built Cray's CDC 6600, gradually moved from the supercomputer field to mainstream business computing and computer consulting, before going out of business altogether before the turn of the millennium.

PART 3

Putting Supercomputers to Work

11

SUPERCOMPUTER CENTERS

The desire for the speed and power of supercomputers keeps super-computer manufacturers in business. But supercomputers are big, expensive machines, and that creates problems. Many more people want to use supercomputers than there are supercomputers for them to use. Gaining access to a supercomputer can be difficult for scientists and other potential users who do not work for a company or an organization with a large budget.

Here is where supercomputer centers come in handy. A supercomputer center acts as a kind of a computing library that loans time on supercomputers to scientists and students, provides information on how to use supercomputers, and promotes supercomputer use. Many supercomputer centers around the world are government-run laboratories; others obtain government grants to buy and run their equipment. Still others combine governmental support with grants from large corporations or industry groups. In return, the centers carry out special assignments and provide computer services free of charge to people who qualify to use them.

At the same time, supercomputer center staff members conduct their own research projects. Much of their work involves seeing how far they can push the performance limits of their machines, either by getting a single supercomputer to perform more work through better programming techniques or by linking computers within and outside

Supercomputer centers such as the National Center for Supercomputing Applications provide access to huge amounts of computing power and sponsor programs to advance the state of the technology. [Courtesy National Center for Supercomputing Applications]

the center to create immense computing networks. By conducting research into the status of computer research, computer scientists are able both to figure out how to use these powerful machines more efficiently and to discover possible improvements that could be incorporated in the design of future supercomputers.

Physically, each center is a cross between an office complex and a university campus. The supercomputers, like any other large mainframe computer system, are kept in large, cooled rooms that are separated from the rest of the building. Elsewhere are facilities such as auditoriums, conference rooms, and classrooms with a large numbers of desktop computers for teaching people how to use supercomputers effectively. There are regular workshops and seminars, and libraries that contain thousands of pages of information and documentation on how to use supercomputers.

The benefits of supercomputer centers go beyond the walls of the buildings that contain their equipment. Naturally, each supercomputer center has its own site on the World Wide Web, as well as newsletters and other informational materials. Gaining access to a supercomputer center often is a matter of linking to its Web site or dialing into its communication network through a dedicated phone line. And supercomputer installations make it as easy as possible for researchers to apply for access to supercomputing facilities, either in person or online.

The National Center for Supercomputing Applications (NCSA) at the University of Illinois at Urbana-Champaign, one of the nation's top supercomputer centers, is a good example of one of these facilities. The NCSA has four supercomputers, the most powerful being an IBM Power4 p690 that can carry out two teraflops, or 2 trillion floating point operations, per second. It performs at this high level with 384 microprocessors, each of which operates at a speed of 1.3 gigahertz (about the same speed as a typical medium-range personal computer), and a memory bank that can hold 1.5 trillion bytes of memory. That machine carries more than double the speed and memory of the NCSA's previous main computer, an Origin2000 system from Silicon Graphics that has 614 gigabytes of memory and used 1,512 processors to achieve a speed of 660 gigaflops.

A Quick World Tour of Supercomputing Institutions

Although supercomputers were developed in the United States, they quickly became an international technology, as shown by the success of companies such as Hitachi and NEC. Several countries besides the United States, including France and Germany as well as Japan, have worked intensely over the past few decades to develop and improve their supercomputing industries. Naturally, where there are supercomputers, there will be supercomputer centers. There are more than 100 supercomputing centers around the world, with the majority located in the United States, Europe, and eastern Asia.

These centers, like their American counterparts, conduct a staggering amount of research. For instance, Taiwan's National Center for High Performance Computing has 15 supercomputers that are put to work on such projects as analyzing the effects of human society and natural disasters on the global environment, refining the field of bioinformatics (the use of computers to manage biological information, such as information about the human genome), and developing computer-aided design systems that could be used to develop prototypes for nanotechnology devices. Japan's supercomputing centers include the Tsukuba Advanced Computing Center, which is maintained by the Japanese Ministry of International Trade and Industry's Agency of Industrial Science and Technology. This high-performance computing institute has a number of supercomputers, including two that ranked among the world's top 50 supercomputers in late 2002. And Finland's Center for Scientific Computing is involved in such research as protein synthesis for creating new drugs, weather analysis, and modeling brain activity.

Some supercomputer centers have gone so far as to build their own supercomputing system, rather than buy one from a supercomputer manufacturer. The Russian Federation's Joint Supercomputer Center, for instance, built a 768-processor system with a theoretical peak performance of 1 trillion floating-point operations per second and a tested speed of 564 gigaflops. Like other types of handmade supercomputing systems, the Joint Supercomputer Center's supercomputers is a cluster of smaller processing units—similar to very high-end personal computers—that are linked with a high-speed communications network. In this case, the network can exchange two gigabits of information a second.

Perhaps the best-known of the supercomputing powerhouses outside the United States, though, is not exactly a supercomputer center. Switzerland's European Laboratory for Particle Physics—better known by its French-language acronym, CERN (which stands for Conseil Européen pour la Recherché Nucléaire)—uses a great amount of supercomputer power to analyze the results of nuclear physics experiments conducted with the facility's huge underground *particle accelerator*. At times, CERN makes its computers available to scientists and engineers in other fields, while its own staff members often find themselves advancing the state of computer technology. The CERN project that had the most visible effect on the world was a simple information-sharing program developed by a computer scientist named Tim Berners-Lee. Lee wanted to create a quick and easy way of gaining access to any document in the network linking CERN's computers with others in Europe. What he designed was a set of *protocols*, or programming rules that determine how computers share information, that became the World Wide Web. (Many of the browsers that people use to pull information off the Web these days are based on Mosaic, a program created at another supercomputer center, the NCSA, by Marc Andreessen.)

But the greatest concentration of supercomputer centers and the greatest concentration of supercomputers are in the United States. According to the November 2002 top-500 supercomputer sites survey of supercomputer use around the world, the United States has 46 percent of the world's highest-performing computers. And seven of the 10 fastest computers in the world are located in America. These results are not surprising: Not only did supercomputers originate in the United States, but so too did the concept of the supercomputer center.

Setting Up Centers in the United States

Supercomputer centers came into being gradually, as the supercomputer industry itself developed. Many centers in the United States got started from the late 1970s to the mid-1980s, having been opened by universities that wanted the machines for research and by large corporations that needed quick access to a lot of computation power. These centers included facilities at Purdue University, the University of Minnesota, Boeing Computer Services, which had been opened by aircraft manufacturer Boeing Company, Digital Productions in Los Angeles, which was a well-known computer animation company during the 1980s, and AT&T Bell Laboratories, which today is known as Lucent Technologies Bell Laboratories.

In the middle of the 1980s, though, the United States faced a couple of technological challenges. The cold war was pushing the development of military technology from tanks to fighter planes, and engineers were relying more and more on high-speed computers to keep ahead of the competition. Supercomputers also were coming online as weapons of analysis, being used for such tasks as cryptology (making and breaking secret codes) and identifying the faint noises submarines make as they travel underwater.

At the same time, Japan's government and its computer industry had set out to create the fifth generation of computing technology. Japanese computer scientists were trying both to create the best computers they could using microprocessors and to develop the circuitry that would replace these microchips, just as transistors had replaced vacuum tubes in the computers of the 1950s. Though the effort never led to the microprocessor's replacement, during the 1980s it was a serious threat to the dominance of American manufacturers over the computer industry in general, and over supercomputers in particular.

To counteract this threat, the U.S. government began supporting and improving America's high-speed computing abilities. The

National Science Foundation (NSF), a federal agency that sponsors research and education programs in all fields of science and engineering, formed the national Office of Advanced Scientific Computing to give university researchers across the nation 22,000 hours of supercomputer time. In 1985 the new office began sponsoring five supercomputer centers: the NCSA, in Urbana, Illinois; the Cornell Theory Center at Cornell University, in Ithaca, New York; the Pittsburgh Supercomputing Center at Carnegie Mellon University, in Pittsburgh, Pennsylvania; the John Von Neumann Center for Scientific Computing, in Princeton, New Jersey (which closed in the early 1990s), and the San Diego Supercomputer Center, at the University of California, San Diego. The NSF also established a computer communication network—NSFNET—that linked the five centers and sponsored secondary networks that connected each center to other universities in their region of the country.

The NSFNET was just one of many computer networks that were put into place in the 1970s and 1980s. The first of these networks, the ARPANET, got its start in the late 1960s under the sponsorship of the U.S. Department of Defense's Advanced Research

The San Diego Supercomputing Center was one of five centers in the United States that were funded by the National Science Foundation in 1985. Here, SDSC researchers examine the active site of reverse transcriptase, a key enzyme from the human immunodeficiency virus. [Courtesy San Diego Supercomputing Center]

Project Agency. As with NSFNET, ARPANET was created as a means to connect researchers with a wide array of computers, more so than they could use at their own universities or research laboratories. And, as with NSFNET, ARPANET had to connect different types of computers in far-flung locations while keeping any delays in transmission to a minimum.

ARPANET's creators solved the communications problems with a combination of specialized hardware, dedicated telephone lines, and programming techniques that connected each computer to every other computer on the network. The computers were connected either directly, with a direct line from one computer to another, or indirectly, with information being transferred through a series of computers until it reached its destination. This method found its way into other computer networks that researchers set up and became the standard communication technique for the modern-day Internet, which itself eventually incorporated the ARPANET into its structure.

NSFNET's creators followed a similar plan to that of the ARPANET, tying all five supercomputer centers together with a primary communication system, or *backbone*, and connecting other computers to this system. The benefits of the NSF program were dramatic. In the supercomputer center network's first five years, the number of researchers who were able to gain access to supercomputers multiplied more than 100 times. By the early 1990s, thousands of scientists from a wide range of fields were able to use the computational power of supercomputers.

At first, scientists were the main group to benefit from the creation of the supercomputer center network. Most of these users were affiliated with universities and other academic or research institutions, and needed the power of supercomputers to conduct research in such varied fields as physics, biochemistry, astronomy, and oceanography. As time went on, the supercomputer centers sought out a wider range of people to use their facilities. Airplane engineers were given the opportunity to conduct computerized wind tunnel tests to analyze the effect of air turbulence along the entire surface of an airplane.

Each supercomputer center also began offering a number of programs for teachers and students who were interested in learning more about computers and supercomputers. Some programs at the San Diego Supercomputer Center (SDSC), for example, were typical of this educational outreach work. SDSC staff members worked with students from the San Diego City Schools Magnet Program, an educational outreach program, to introduce them to computers in general and to the things that could be done with supercomputers. For elementary and middle school teachers, the SDSC offered a Supercomputing Teacher Enhancement Program (STEP). The activities included hands-on training sessions, weekend "Discover Science" sessions for teachers, and guided tours of the SDSC. And the SDSC staff helped schools evaluate their science education programs and gauge the quality of the computing equipment and other technology that their students were using.

The other NSF-sponsored centers started similar programs. The National Center for Supercomputing Applications (NCSA) put together a high-school-level summer program called SuperQuest that gave students hands-on experience with supercomputers and exposed them to advanced forms of computational science. To be admitted to the program, a team of three or four students and their teacher had to submit a proposal for a science project that they would conduct at the NCSA. These projects required supercomputer assistance with complex mathematical equations, including studies of how populations change over time, of automobile aerodynamics, and of predator-prey relationships in the wild.

Supercomputer centers also benefited universities, especially those that host the centers. At the University of Illinois at Urbana-Champaign's Renaissance Experimental Laboratory, located in the university's Beckman Institute, faculty members who taught computer graphics in their courses could use laboratory workstations connected to the NCSA to assist them in their work. Courses were available in subjects such as biophysics, computer science, mathematics, chemistry, art, and design.

The four NSF supercomputer sites were not the only ones of their kind. The success of the federally supported supercomputer centers prompted other universities to start their own facilities, often with support from state legislatures and grants from corporations and private foundations. These sites conducted the same types of research and provided the same computing services that the NSF centers made available. However, the NSF program was seen as a trend-setting force in the world of high-speed computing.

Promoting the Use of Supercomputers

The four supercomputer centers that the National Science Foundation sponsored were only one part of the government's effort to improve supercomputing. Toward the end of 1991, President George H.W. Bush signed the High Performance Computing Act to accelerate the development of supercomputers and link them to universities, laboratories, and private companies throughout the nation. This legislation allowed the NSF to revise the communications network that connected the five supercomputer centers and create a more efficient way to use their resources.

Called the National MetaCenter for Computational Science and Engineering, the program linked the San Diego, Cornell, Pittsburgh, and Urbana-Champaign supercomputing centers with an improved communications network. Unlike the NSFNET system, which was tied into a dedicated *backbone* (central communications system), the Meta-Center network tied into the Internet, which the general public was discovering and learning how to use. The new organization gave scientists the ability to use a greater amount of supercomputer power from their university workstations or from their own desktop computers.

Another benefit of the MetaCenter was its ability to help large teams of researchers from many fields of science work together to solve extremely complex and difficult problems known as grand-challenge problems. A grand-challenge problem generally involves the attempt to prove a seemingly impossible scientific hypothesis or engineer a cutting-edge mechanism. Examples of this type of research include identifying how the theories of physics apply to the everyday workings of biological systems and creating workable nanotechnology devices.

The MetaCenter played a role in testing new computer configurations to learn which were most useful in helping scientists with their research and which produced the most valuable kinds of information. This function was an extension of one of the original goals of the supercomputer center program, which was to spur the development of more powerful supercomputers and supercomputing techniques. And the MetaCenter's creators planned to establish a national file and archival storage system along with a high-speed network dedicated to its use. Using local supercomputers connected to the MetaCenter, researchers would be able to pull files of data or analyses from the national storage system for use in their projects. The MetaCenter network would transfer data within the system linking the four main supercomputer centers.

Unfortunately, this grand dream was cut short in favor of a set of more ambitious projects. In a way, the problem was one of technological success. The NSF Supercomputers Center Program, including NSFNET and the MetaCenter, lasted until well into the 1990s, but in time it was outpaced by rapid advances in computing. The goal of the original supercomputer centers—to give researchers the ability to gain access to supercomputers from their desktops—was something that seemed truly remarkable in the early-to-mid-1980s. (Remember, these were the days before the Internet boom of the 1990s, when desktop computers still were a novelty. Computing online meant dialing into a university mainframe or a community *bulletin board system* with a modem that transferred information at maybe 4,500 bits per second.) With the development of high-speed Internet access, the World Wide Web, and better computers in general, the supercomputer program found that its main goal had been accomplished.

The four original NSF supercomputing centers still are in operation, with their operating funds coming from a combination of grants from federal and state government agencies, corporations, and a few private organizations. They continue to provide computing muscle for researchers whose projects require it, and they continue to promote the use of supercomputing in a wide array of subjects. However, in 1997 the NSF changed the way in which it supported supercomputing projects. It replaced its 12-year-old Supercomputer Center Program with a new research agenda called Partnerships for Advanced Computational Infrastructure, or PACI. PACI's goal is to harness the power of computers throughout the World Wide Web into a "computer-mediated center of knowledge," creating a massive, online research domain that anyone can tap into from any computer. Known as the National Technology Grid, the PACI program would link more than 50 sites, mainly university computer centers and scientific research facilities.

PACI itself contains two programs that are headed by two of the original four supercomputer centers. The NCSA is home to the National Computational Science Alliance, often called simply the Alliance, while the SDSC is the headquarters of the National Partnership for an Advanced Computational Infrastructure, or NPACI. Both programs have essentially the same goal: to develop an Internet-based computing network called the Grid that would link supercomputers, scientific laboratories, informational databases, and groups of researchers. Both supercomputer centers are working with a group of more than 50 universities, government organizations, and corporations that would benefit from the network.

At the same time, the NSF is sponsoring another scientific computing program that will harness a host of supercomputers in a scientific research super-network with a titanic amount of computing power. Called TeraGrid, the new network will provide access to 20 teraflops' worth of computing power—20 trillion, or 20 million million, operations per second—tied together with a communications system that will be able to transfer 40 gigabits of data per second.

All this computing power will be distributed at five supercomputer sites. Three of them are original NSF supercomputer centers: NCSA, SDSC, and the Pittsburgh Supercomputer Center. The other two are well-established supercomputer facilities in their own right: the Center for Advanced Computing Research at the California Institute of Technology in Pasadena, a city to the northeast of Los Angeles, and the Argonne National Laboratory in Illinois.

When the TeraGrid and the National Technology Grid start operating, researchers undoubtedly will use it to work on the types of grand challenge projects that the old MetaCenter program was designed to help solve. But other projects that run on these grids may be similar to the work that researchers are conducting on supercomputers today.

12

SUPERCOMPUTERS AND SCIENCE

From their earliest days, supercomputers have been science machines, designed for researchers who need a high-speed number-crunching machine that can help make sense of their experimental data. The first Control Data Corporation CDC 6600 computer, whose creation kicked off the supercomputer era, went to the Lawrence Livermore Radiation Laboratory (later renamed the Lawrence Livermore National Laboratory), a government-run nuclear energy and weapons research facility in the San Francisco Bay area of California. There, scientists used it to decipher data from experiments in atomic physics and to run simulations of nuclear warhead designs. From that point on, Lawrence Livermore and other government facilities were constant customers for supercomputer manufacturers, with university and industrial labs quickly signing orders for their own machines.

As promised, supercomputers dramatically slashed the time it took to run experiments and analyze data. Researchers around the world dreamed of being able to use these high-speed calculating dynamos, and they envied the few scientists who actually had access to one. Supercomputers became status symbols for the laboratories and universities that owned them, and often became part of the recruiting effort when these institutions sought to attract new researchers.

These days, supercomputers have become the go-to machines for much of modern science, and the fastest supercomputers each year are the ones used for scientific applications. Actually, researchers could not have made many of their discoveries since the 1980 without the assistance of supercomputers. Phenomena that are extremely large and complex—such as weather or astronomical interactions—or are extremely small—such as the makeup of new materials or genetics—cannot be recreated in a standard laboratory. Instead, scientists use supercomputers as laboratories in which they simulate conditions such as these and as tools to analyze the huge amounts of data that these and other experiments generate.

Making Sense of Turbulence

Events that involve the rapid flow and mixture of gases or liquids—in other words, turbulence—are some of the most difficult phenomena to study. Predicting the exact effects of turbulence caused by the flow of air over an airplane wing, by a propeller as it pushes a ship through the water, or by two weather fronts as they collide is almost impossible. The best that scientists and engineers can do is mathematically estimate how turbulent flow might develop. They create these estimates using *calculus*, the branch of mathematics that deals with how one quantity, such as wind speed, varies in relation to others, such as location or time of day.

Meteorologists, scientists who study and predict the weather, deal with turbulence as a routine part of their work. The problem with predicting weather, as well as with studying climate patterns, is change. Weather is the result of the interaction between different forces such as atmospheric pressure, the energy from sunlight, air temperature, and even the rotation of the Earth. Although meteorologists know the laws that govern the physical world, they have their hands full tracking all the changes that take place according to these laws. Even using programs based on advanced calculus, meteorologists need the power of supercomputers to generate a timely estimate of what the skies will do over a set of days.

The type of weather forecasts that appear on the evening news do not require the aid of supercomputers, as most workstations can handle the calculations needed to figure out the weather up to a week in the future. Instead, supercomputers come into play for studying why the weather behaves as it does and determining long-range weather trends.

Meteorologists use calculus to represent the interactions that take place across the surface of the Earth or within the body of a tornado-generating storm. In weather studies, for example, researchers divide a portion of Earth's surface into a three-dimensional grid that includes *data points* on the ground and at specified altitudes. The scientists then measure temperature, humidity, wind speed, wind direction, soil moisture, and any other factor at each data point that can influence how the atmosphere behaves. Using this information, the scientists program their supercomputers to simulate the way weather varies with latitude, longitude, and altitude. The mathematical models they use account for the roiling, turbulent interactions between air masses, *frontal systems*, and the winds they generate, all of which are represented by different equations.

Accurate weather forecasting also involves analyzing data from large-scale and small-scale weather events. Large-scale phenomena, such as *jet streams*, take place over hundreds of square miles and at many levels in the atmosphere. Jet streams constantly weave far to the north or south as they blow across the globe, causing dramatic shifts in local weather. At the same time, small-scale events such as *squall lines*, tornadoes, and *wind shear* can interfere with or support the effects caused by large-scale weather events. All of these interacting forces and conditions combine to create a mind-numbing mass of data that requires a computer to handle.

Of course, the result of a supercomputer's work can also be mind-numbing—graphs comparing one set of weather data to another, or long lists of numbers detailing the force of air pressure or wind speed changes. Fortunately, supercomputers also provide the means for creating a better type of visual presentation. Weather analyses can take the form of simple two-dimensional maps of an area being studied or complex, computer-generated movies showing how a thunderstorm develops. At the National Center for Atmospheric Research in Boulder, Colorado, meteorologists have even been experimenting with *stereoscopic* computer-graphic models as tools for analyzing and predicting weather phenomena. These types of displays could help scientists make important new discoveries that might not have been made any other way.

Bringing the Stars Down to Earth

Astronomers, astrophysicists, and other space scientists routinely run experiments on supercomputers as they search for possible explanations of how the universe formed. One of the biggest pieces of this overall puzzle is the mystery of how material in the early universe formed itself into galaxies. The evidence seems to support two contrasting theories, which for the sake of simplicity are called the "bottom-up" and the "top-down" theories. The "bottom-up" theory states that galaxies started as relatively small structures: dense, cold clouds of gas that gradually gathered more material and warmed up under the influence of increased pressure and gravity (known as a *protogalaxy*). Eventually, these small protogalaxies ("proto-" meaning "before or first in time") developed into galaxies, which drifted together to form galaxy clusters and *superclusters*, or clusters of galactic clusters.

The "top-down" theory, on the other hand, states that superclusters of gas, dust, and other materials formed first, then fragmented into individual galaxies. A Russian scientist, Yakob B. Zel'dovich, speculated that the early superclusters of material would collapse, most probably into a flattened structure that he described as a pancake. Zel'dovich's theory predicted that the collapse would cause the material to fragment into galaxies because of gravitational instability—titanic clumps of dust within the "pancake" would pull less-dense fields of material into themselves, forming protogalaxies.

Dr. Wenbo Y. Anninos, a researcher at NCSA in the early 1990s, explored the "top-down" theory by using a supercomputer programmed with an astrophysics software tool called ZEUS-2D. The software was able to generate two-dimensional visual simulations of galaxies, gas clouds, and other structures that form in space. To simulate the collapse and fragmentation that Zel'dovich predicted, Anninos created a model of the gases and other material from which the galaxies would have formed, including mathematical representations of density, pressure, temperature, and the expansion of the universe.

"The simulation had been done in one dimension before and demonstrated the collapse, but they could not observe fragmentation," Anninos said. With the two-dimensional simulation, though, she was able to show both the fragmentation of Zel'dovich's "pancake" and the formation of protogalaxies from the fragments. While this work did not prove that the "top-down" theory was correct, it added to the evidence in favor on this model of how galaxies came into being.

Another major area of astronomical research is the study of *black holes, supernovas*, and the gravitational waves these phenomena create. Astrophysicists believe that black holes are the remains of ancient stars that have collapsed into extremely dense masses of stellar material, with gravitational fields so powerful that even light cannot escape their influence. Supernovas, on the other hand, are stars that explode with enough power to vaporize any planets that may be orbiting them and create a surge of light and other radiation that briefly outshine any other star.

Albert Einstein, the theoretical physicist who devised the general and special theories of relativity, defined gravity as a variation caused by any object in the three-dimensional fabric of space. A way to imagine this effect is to think of a softball sitting in the center of a tight bedsheet. The dip in the sheet would represent a portion of the softball's gravitational field. Einstein also theorized that cataclysmic events, such as a supernova's explosion or a collision between black holes, would send gravitational waves through the universe, much as an explosion sends shock waves through the atmosphere. As these gravitational waves passed around Earth, Einstein said, they could be detected with an extremely sensitive detector.

In the 1980s the U.S. government paid for the construction of two special observatories that use lasers to detect the passage of these gravitational waves. The laser beam's emitters and their detectors are separated by a large enough distance for the detector to register the tiny movements caused by the passing waves. Once the observatory was in place, identifying the origin of each wave and the circumstances that created it was a straightforward matter. Just as each person has a unique fingerprints and handwriting, each gravitational wave has unique *signature*, a set of characteristics that make it different from others.

Ed Seidel, a researcher at the NCSA in the early 1990s, used supercomputer power to create a catalog of gravitational wave signatures to help other researchers identify the sources of waves they detect. The reason he needed a supercomputer for this work was to handle the complex mathematics needed to describe the force of each type of wave. "Most systems have a normal 'mode frequency,' just like a bell," Seidel said. "If you hit a bell, it rings with a certain frequency. Different-sized bells have different frequencies. Black holes also have special frequencies, only the wave being propagated is a gravitational wave."

Studying and Shaping Matter's Building Blocks

During the Middle Ages, alchemists tried to transform *base metals* such as lead into gold using mystical formulas and exotic materials, none of

Heike Kamerlingh Onnes, shown here in his laboratory, discovered the phenomenon of superconductivity in mercury in 1911. [Photo from the Rijksmuseum Voor de Geschiedenis der Natuurwetenschappen te Leiden; Courtesy American Institute of Physics, Emilio Segrè Visual Archives]

which worked. Modern scientists, though, have been trying to design new materials with the assistance of supercomputers. One particularly intense area of materials research is high-temperature *superconductors*, materials that can carry electrical charges with little or no resistance. Superconductors have been suggested as the basis for more efficient electrical power and generation, new types of electronic devices, and even supercomputers that operate at even faster speeds than those available today.

Superconductivity has been known since 1911, when Dutch scientist Heike Kamerlingh Onnes was studying how very cold temperatures affected how metals conduct electricity. One of the metals Onnes tested was mercury, which he cooled to a temperature of roughly –269 degrees Celsius (–452 degrees Fahrenheit) in a bath of liquid helium. As it turned out, the current passed through the supercooled mercury without any loss in strength. This result was astounding: while physicists knew in those days that cold metals conducted electricity better than warm ones, they thought any material that would conduct electricity would provide at least some amount of resistance. Onnes and other researchers soon discovered a range of metals that also exhibited this process of superconductivity when cooled in liquid helium.

Unfortunately, it was so expensive to maintain such extremely cold temperatures that Onnes's discovery was of little practical importance. Though physicists sought superconductors that operated at higher temperatures for the next 70 years, no significant improvements over Onnes's work occurred until 1983. That was when two researchers who worked for IBM in Zurich, Switzerland—K. Alexander Müller and J. George Bednorz—decided to try working with a class of ceramics called *perovskites* that behaves somewhat like metals.

The researchers tested hundreds of perovskite samples over the next three years before hitting upon a ceramic mixture that became superconducting at –245 degrees Celsius (–409 degrees Fahrenheit). Though this temperature is still too cold to be practical, the discovery was a breakthrough in its own right, and a worldwide race began to find materials that would act as superconductors at higher and higher temperatures. The first goal in this race was to find a superconductor that would operate at –196 degrees Celsius (about –321 degrees Fahrenheit), a temperature at which liquid nitrogen—a far less expensive coolant than liquid helium—could be used.

In January 1987, two physicists, Dr. Paul Chu and Dr. Maw-Kuen Wu, went above this "magic threshold" and achieved superconductivity at a temperature above –183 degrees Celsius (–297 degrees Fahrenheit). The superconducting material they used was an oxide of the metals yttrium, barium, and copper. A year later, researchers at the University of Arkansas discovered another compound that superconducted at –148 degrees Celsius (–234 degrees Fahrenheit). Since then, scientists have been seeking a substance that will superconduct at 27 degrees Celsius (80 degrees Fahrenheit). At this temperature, no special coolants would be needed and superconductivity could be used for many everyday applications.

The problem with creating these high-temperature superconductors has been the general air of mystery in which these materials operate. Even though scientists have been able to create superconducting ceramics and have theorized why they work, they do not truly understand why they work, or what exactly happens to these materials when they go from normal to cooled states. Studying the behavior of high-temperature superconductors has meant creating detailed mathematical models of the materials and, again mathematically, studying them

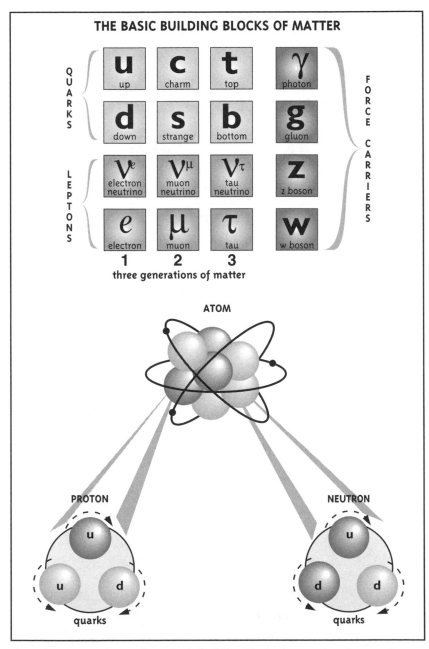

These drawings represent the 16 basic building blocks that are thought to make up all matter and that control how matter interacts. Physicists have used supercomputers to collect and analyze data about the behavior of these particles. The words *up, down, charm, strange, top,* and *bottom* are terms physicists use to describe the spin and other properties of quarks.

from moment to moment as they cool to their superconductive states. Such calculations can only take place on a supercomputer that can follow these changes on a nanosecond-to-nanosecond basis.

Grinding through the Genome

One of the most intensive applications of supercomputers to biology took place in the last decade of the 20th century, during a worldwide project to decipher the human *genome*. Each living thing on Earth— fungus, plant, or animal—carries within its cells a collection of molecules that pass on the chemical codes, or *genes*, that determine form and function. The genome is the arrangement of all the codes that make up an organism's genetic blueprint. The molecules that contain these codes, *deoxyribonucleic acid* (DNA) and *ribonucleic acid* (RNA), are long, though tiny, structures made up of smaller molecules called *nucleotides*. Each nucleotide, in turn, consists of a sugar, a type of molecule called a phosphate group, and a chemical called a *base*.

DNA and RNA both have four bases, three of which they have in common: *adenine* (A), *cytosine* (C), and *guanine* (G). The fourth base in DNA is *thymine* (T), while the fourth base in RNA is *uracil* (U). Only

Combining supercomputers with genetic sequencers such as these has allowed scientists to map the genomes of human beings and other species. [Courtesy of Oak Ridge National Laboratory]

one of these bases may be part of each nucleotide. In DNA two strands of nucleotides wrap together in a *helix*, with the bases of each strand pairing up across the helix in a specific way: adenine with thymine, and cytosine with guanine.

The chemical codes called genes actually are sequences of three nucleotide bases along the DNA molecule that tell cells how to create protein molecules, which are the workhorse molecules of life. Proteins often are called muscle-building nutrients, because the muscles contain especially high amounts of various proteins. However, proteins perform many other tasks. Different protein molecules can serve as antibodies, which fight infections; as enzymes, the biological catalysts that start or speed up chemical reactions; or as part of the structure of a cell's wall.

For decades, biologists and medical researchers looked at the human genome the way that space scientists looked at the Moon and the planet Mars: as both a goal to be reached and as a starting point for future discoveries. Mapping all the genes present in human beings—that is, locating the genes on their specific chromosomes—would lead to new insights into treating hereditary diseases. In addition, this might lead to medical revolutions, such as custom-tailored pharmaceutical drugs or specially grown replacement limbs for people who lose arms or legs from an accident. Such advances would eliminate many problems, such as drug side effects or the rejection of surgical transplants.

In the early 1990s researchers in the United States started the Human Genome Project, an effort to create this genetic map that swiftly grew into an international race to decipher the DNA code. Prestige and the potential for licensing this knowledge to drug makers and other researchers drew interest from beyond the public sector. Private companies competed with government-sponsored labs to prepare the first full guide to the human blueprint. As work progressed, it became clear that the Human Genome Project could not have been carried out without supercomputers. Geneticists used supercomputers to control gene sequencers, the machines that separated and analyzed the thousands of DNA samples collected for the project. Supercomputers also were given the task of arranging and storing the information as it came out of the sequencers, along with the many variations in the code that appeared from sample to sample.

When the Human Genome Project got under way in 1990s, the most optimistic experts figured it would take at least 15 years to reach the goal of a fully sequenced genome. As new research groups joined the scientific race, though, they brought in better equipment as well as better knowledge of the subject, thanks to the work of earlier researchers. At the turn of the millennium, scientists at the private firm Celera Genomics, which had started work in 1998 with a supercomputer built by Compaq, announced that they had completed the quest for the genome, a mere decade after the Human Genome Project began.

Supercomputers and Computer Science

In addition to helping researchers push the boundaries of scientific knowledge, supercomputers continue to serve as tools for improving the state of modern computing. Microprocessors continually come out with more and more transistors packed onto fingernail-sized semiconductor chips. However, before those transistors find their way onto those chips, someone has to figure out exactly where the transistors, and the circuitry that connects them, will go.

Designing a new microprocessor is sort of like drawing up a city road map, with transistors at each intersection. Electrons must be able to travel through the system without colliding or suddenly being switched to a different route. Making the task harder is the knowledge that the final layout will be reproduced thousands, if not millions, of times. Any mistakes that make their way into the final design will be part of that chip forever.

Keeping track of all the circuit paths, their interchanges, and the points where they pass over and under each other is an exercise in microscopic traffic control. Computer-assisted circuit design software makes this work easier for the men and women who engineer new *microchips*. However, until recently the task of checking microcircuits for errors literally brought chip designers to their knees. Crawling over gigantic drawings of the proposed processors, the engineers would trace each circuit from beginning to end.

Supercomputers have taken over this ordeal at most microchip manufacturers. Programmed with the completed circuit layout, a supercomputer will function as a high-speed map editor, running through every route on the chip and identifying those with problems. As a result, manufacturers have been able to improve their chips and create new microprocessors at a rate equal to or faster than those of the past, despite the presence of millions of transistors on each new processor.

Supercomputers and Simulation

Computers have been used to simulate real-world events from the days of the vacuum-tube, first-generation machines such as EDVAC and UNIVAC. The Whirlwind computer that formed the core of the early-warning SAGE system was a real-time simulation of the skies over the United States. Even computers that run some strictly math-based programs, with no visual output, can be considered simulation systems of the program is sufficiently complex.

However, since the mid-1980s, scientists have been using increasingly sophisticated methods for analyzing experimental data using detailed two-dimensional and three-dimensional computer graphics. The most advanced of these systems can present their information as interactive, *stereoscopic* displays that allow scientists to view and manipulate data from nearly any perspective. Some of the weather analysis projects at NCAR, as well as similar projects at other research facilities, have been set up to take advantage of this technology in the analysis of such events as wildfires and hurricanes.

For projects such as these, in fact, supercomputers actually make the scientific method easier to follow. Science is a six-stage process for analyzing and explaining natural phenomena. The first stage is observation: taking note of a physical, biological, or chemical process. Next comes deduction: basically, estimating the reason why the process takes place and setting up a theory to explore in the third stage, experimentation. The fourth and fifth stages of science involve determining if the results of the experiment support the theory and, if necessary, changing the theory to fit the results. The final stage involves repeating the experiment to see if the same results come out.

Supercomputer simulations make it easier to conduct and repeat large experiments, and to analyze the data the experiments yield. Since all of the elements of the original experiment can be saved in a series of computer files, it is a simple matter to repeat the simulation under conditions that are identical to the first run. And with the power of a supercomputer at hand, scientists can easily compare different sets of data to find if the results of a particular experiment are consistent.

SUPERCOMPUTERS AND INDUSTRIAL DESIGN

Industrial design is the combination of engineering and art that goes into the creation of products as simple as furniture and as mechanically complicated as satellites. Whatever industry they are in, companies want their goods to be inexpensive to make and easy to sell, while offering their customers reasonable levels of reliability, safety, and ease of use. At the same time, each company constantly seeks ways to set its products apart from those of its competitors, whether through a unique appearance or through a higher level of quality.

This process takes a lot of effort, and there is always a risk that a flaw will slip past the many people who review and double-check this work. Manufacturers have been using computers to help make this process faster and more accurate ever since 1959. That year, General Motors Corporation engineers began using a system called Design Augmented by Computers, or DAC-1, that the automaker and IBM had developed. The first example of what came to be called *computer-aided design*, DAC-1 used a high-speed computer and a computer-controlled charting table to analyze automobile designs and draw up plans for construction.

As computers got faster and computer graphics became more sophisticated, manufacturers in many industries adopted computer-aided design, which became known by its acronym, CAD. The growth of the supercomputer field led to highly sophisticated CAD systems that could create three-dimensional models of products as detailed as airplanes and automobiles, complete with engines and other mechanical structures. Even better, the supercomputers could analyze how these products would perform in the real world, such as gauging airflow over an airplane's wing. As expected, industrial designers and engineers who used CAD in their work found they could reduce the time it took them to find problems and prepare the product's final plans.

By the end of the 20th century, corporations around the world were using supercomputers to enhance the design process of products ranging from automobiles to athletic shoes. Even noncommercial products, such as the space shuttle, received the benefits of supercomputer-aided design. Researchers with the National Aeronautics and Space Administration (NASA) used supercomputer simulations to correct a problem with the shuttle's fuel delivery system. Ducts that carried hydrogen fuel into the combustion chamber of the shuttle's engines bent at severe angles, enough in some places to restrict the fuel's flow and reduce the amount of thrust the engines could provide. Scientists at NASA's Ames Research Center in northern California analyzed the problem using a supercomputer re-creation of the shuttle engines and corrected the angles of the ducts to yield better performance.

Also in the 1990s, aerospace companies competed for contracts to develop a proposed hypersonic spacecraft that could take off and land like a conventional airplane, yet reach orbit like a space shuttle. The hope of this project was to create a ground-to-space vehicle that would be more efficient and more economical to operate than the space shuttle, and thus make it possible to schedule more space flights. Researchers at Rockwell International, one of the companies involved in this work, said it would have been impossible to consider such a concept without the power of supercomputer computation.

A Brainstorming Tool in a Desktop Box

When designers use a supercomputer, they do not interact directly with the supercomputer's huge collection of processors. They interact with a very powerful desktop unit much like a personal computer that communicates with the supercomputer, or even with one that is a supercomputer in itself. Such types of superpowered computers are called *workstations* and contain more computing power than supercomputers that were considered top-of-the-line machines as recently as 15 years ago.

In addition to car and airplane manufacturers, special-effects companies used workstations to create computer-generated images and animation for the entertainment industry, and some researchers used these computers to create scientific images, such as the structure of molecules. Extra-large monitors and other accessories helped make the work even easier, but the amazing feat was the amount of work the workstation could do. Until supercomputers became inexpensive enough, these computers did an adequate job of filling the gap. Whether they used large supercomputers or small workstations with nearly supercomputer-level power in their industrial applications, though, designers quickly discovered that the great advance of working with computer assistance was the ability to change plans on the fly.

Without supercomputers, or even high-powered desktop computers, designers and engineers have to spend hours making all but the simplest changes in, for example, the body of a family sedan. Changing the shape of a car's hood or the lines of its trunk lid can affect fuel efficiency on the freeway or even how well the car protects its occupants during a collision. Changes such as these require a recalculation of how well the design would bear up to real-world conditions or, at the very least, the reworking of the plans that finally determine how the car will be built.

With supercomputers, the task becomes much easier. Just as writers can change sentences and paragraphs using word-processing programs, engineers and designers can alter appearances, substitute parts, and even change entire structures with a few simple commands. The supercomputers take over the task of calculating how these changes will affect the final design, and in some cases can generate three-dimensional images for group discussion and input as well as two-dimensional plans.

As a result, manufacturers have been able to drastically reduce much of the process of manufacturing. Updating or replacing existing products are tasks that now can be measured in months, rather than years. And gaining an advantage over a business rival is becoming as much a matter of better computing as it is of better advertising.

On-screen Prototypes and Instant Models

Airplane manufacturers are in a very competitive business. Their products are expected to last for at least 20 years of nearly continuous operation, while costing their owners the least amount of money possible to fly and maintain. In order to attract buyers, each manufacturer has to design its airplanes to achieve the lowest sales price, the greatest fuel efficiency, and the easiest maintenance schedule that can be developed. At the same time, each airplane design—especially those for passenger airplanes—has to meet strict safety standards. Keeping these and other matters in mind is a daunting task, even with the aid of supercomputers.

Of all these factors, the ones that drive the airplane design process are fuel efficiency and airspeed. The reasons are simple: Fuel efficiency determines how far an airplane can go on a load of fuel, and airspeed determines how quickly the plane can get there. Naturally, there are trade-offs between these two aspects of airplane performance, and between these and the other features of the aircraft. A small, propeller-driven passenger plane, for example, may use less fuel and travel farther on the same amount of fuel than a medium-sized jetliner. However, the jet plane will be able to travel faster and with a larger number of paying passengers.

Manufacturers also need to know the maximum physical limits that a proposed airplane design can withstand while in flight. Typically, the development of a commercial or a military airplane involves testing scale models of proposed airplane designs, or airframes, in *wind tunnels* that simulate real-world flight conditions. In the wind tunnel, the airplane model experiences the many physical forces that the full-sized airframe would face. Manufacturers can find out how fast and how easily the airframe can climb and turn, even the point at which the craft might stall.

If the model is successful, the manufacturer builds a *prototype*, a full-size, working model of the airplane. Test pilots take on the dangerous tasks of flying these prototypes to uncover any problems with the design that the wind tunnel tests do not pick up. For example, an engine may not perform as well as expected or a wing surface may start fluttering under stresses that the wind-tunnel model did not experience.

As necessary as wind-tunnel tests were, building wind tunnels and running experiments with model aircraft is an expensive and time-consuming process. That is why aeronautical engineers and airplane manufacturers have turned to supercomputers as an alternative to the decades-old testing method. Supercomputers offer many ways to simulate aircraft designs and the flying conditions they might face.

One of the major enemies of fuel economy is the friction created as the airplane pushes aside the air molecules in its path. Airplanes fly because of lift generated from air flowing faster over the top of a wing than beneath it. The faster airflow creates a zone of low-pressure air that pushes down on the wing with a force weaker than the air pushing up on the wing's underside. But the air molecules do not slide over the wing's surface or over the rest of the airplane's structure, like a water drop over a sheet of Teflon. Instead, the air drags against and bounces off these surfaces, creating turbulence and adding to the effort that the plane's engines must exert to keep the plane in the air.

Engineers, scientists, and pilots alike have known about drag since the earliest days of human flight. Decades of wind-tunnel tests showed the presence of drag and helped aeronautical engineers reduce its effects, but the exact areas where drag was worst remained undetectable until supercomputers came into the industry. Engineers with the Boeing Company were among the first to use supercomputers for a solely industrial task. With the computational power of supercomputers, they were able to examine airflow patterns over an airplane's wings and body at a level of detail never before possible. They also turned the plans for the plane into a three-dimensional graphic image of the airframe and the flow patterns that could be viewed from any angle.

One of the first commercial jet aircraft to be analyzed using a supercomputer, the Boeing 737, had been in service for 20 years despite a well-known problem with excessive drag. Boeing's engineers had long suspected that the drag problems stemmed from the way the craft's engines attached to the wings. Jet engines hang beneath a jetliner's wings on a strut called a *pylon* to prevent interference between the airflow over the wing's upper surface and the airflow through the engine. However, the supercomputer analysis showed that the way the 737's engine had been mounted—close to the underside of the wing but leaving a gap between the engine and the wing—as well as the shape of the casing around the engine were causing the excessive drag that had plagued the aircraft.

By using these findings, and by using supercomputer analyses of many new design ideas, Boeing's engineers solved both these problems. They designed a new casing for the engine, one that allowed air to slip by with less friction, and mounted the engine directly onto the wing of the 737 in a way that avoided interfering with the flow of air

Boeing Company used supercomputers to design its wide bodied 777-200 airliner, which did not exist in physical form until the first test model rolled out of the construction hangar. [Courtesy Boeing Company]

over the wing. These two simple design changes improved the aircraft's performance so dramatically that Boeing decided to apply supercomputer analysis to an entirely new airliner, the wide-bodied 777-200, so named because it was the successor to the 767 and it could accommodate 200 passengers.

When it rolled out in the spring of 1994, the 777-200 was the world's largest twin-jet airliner. Boeing had asked its customers—airline companies in the United States and around the world—what they wanted in such a large-capacity airplane. The airlines' responses resulted in more than 1,000 design changes to the proposed plans for the 777-200 that would make the airplane less expensive to build, operate, and service, as well as more appealing to passengers. Normally, such a number of changes would have meant months, if not years, of work by engineers, draftsmen, and others on the airplane's design team. However, making the changes to the 777-200's plans was easy, as they were all stored in easy-to-alter graphics files on computer.

The 777-200's engineers had not used supercomputers merely to analyze and double-check the results of wind-tunnel tests. They had designed the entire aircraft, from passenger cabin to rudder controls, with computers. They analyzed the structure of the 777-200, looked over the placement of its seats and windows, fitted its engines, and set up its cockpit simply by looking at computer-graphic images on monitor screens. In fact, until working test-flight versions of the airplane rolled down the runway at Boeing's Seattle, Washington, test facility, the design existed solely in the circuits of Boeing's supercomputer and on a few sets of plans printed off from the computer files. Creating the 777-200 this way not only shortened the time it took to build the plane but dramatically cut the cost of designing the craft.

The success of the 777-200 design was a triumph of aeronautical engineering that was years in arriving. William F. Ballhaus Jr., a former director of the NASA Ames Research Center and an early advocate of using supercomputers for airplane design, once said that several airplane designs would have been much better with the aid of supercomputers. Among these were such well-known military cargo planes as the C-5A Galaxy, the C-141 Starlifter, and the F-111 Aardvark fighter/bomber, which was notorious for its design flaws in its early years. The initial designs of these and other airplanes had problems such as incorrect airflow over the wings or unexpected drag that appeared only at or near the speed of sound. Often, engineers and test pilots learned of these flaws during the first few test flights. In each case, these problems led to expensive redesign work, production delays, less efficient performance, and a shortened service life for these planes before advances in technology forced their replacement.

Manufacturing Made More Efficient

In the 20 years after General Motors began using its DAC-1 system to design automobiles, carmakers picked up on the idea of using computer-aided design systems. By the mid-1980s most of the work of creating new vehicles involved the use of computer-aided design systems, allowing engineers to create three-dimensional objects on two-dimensional computer displays. At the same time, the CAD files that contained the revised designs often went directly to the factory floor. In addition to CAD, automakers and other manufacturers developed *computer-assisted machinery*, or CAM, systems that turn the computerized designs into a series of assembly commands for robotic tools. The robot arms that do much of the welding on automobile assembly lines are an example of CAM systems at work. Automatic cutting tools that fabricate parts out of sheet metal or metal blocks are other examples.

However, as with airplane design, the process of car design also requires car manufacturers to build full-sized prototypes of the cars being developed, as a way to view how the final product would look in a dealership's showroom. Sculptors create clay models of each car's exterior and interior, based on the designers' plans; other workers make full-size fiberglass mock-ups of the car based on these models, creating a complete vehicle body for the automaker's managers to examine and approve for production.

Engineers analyze the design of a small car using a virtual-reality display powered by a supercomputer. This type of collaborative computing is finding its way into the offices of many car companies. [Courtesy Opticore Corp.]

Adding supercomputers to the automotive engineer's toolkit has made this job easier. Today, all parts of an automobile can be simulated in the circuits of a supercomputer. Factors such as airflow, noise, vibrations, and stresses to a car's structure can be applied to the computerized model of the car's design. As this information flows through the supercomputer's circuits, it helps reveal not only where problems exist but also where materials or parts can be eliminated to make assembling the car easier without compromising its safety or reliability.

Often, measures to improve manufacturing efficiency also make the car more economical to use. Improving the performance of internal combustion engines to save fuel is an important part of automobile design, both for attracting potential buyers and for meeting federal pollution and energy-consumption standards. Two ways to increase fuel efficiency are to improve the combustion of gasoline in the engine and, as with airplanes, to reduce the aerodynamic drag caused by the flow of air over the automobile's body as it travels.

Studying the complex actions and interactions of forces that take place within car engines has always been a matter of mathematical visualization. It is impossible to see what happens inside an engine while it is working, so engineers have had to make do with measuring pressure, temperature, and other forces and estimating what goes on during the combustion cycle. Supercomputers, though, can use programs that contain the rules of physics as they apply to engine operations and simulate how engine designs would work under various conditions. By studying how well the digital engines work, engineers can adjust their designs to create a final motor that works more effectively than it otherwise would have.

Supercomputer simulations also have helped researchers craft automobile exteriors that create the least amount of drag, especially at high speed. These simulations have been used to study every exposed part and surface of an automobile. In the mid-1990s, for example, two engineers at the Institute of Computational Fluid Dynamics in Tokyo conducted a supercomputer study of airflow around the tires of a simulated automobile and how the flow affects the performance of the rest of the car. They discovered that the spinning tires stirred the air enough to create turbulence at the rear of the car, creating a slight low-pressure zone that would act as a sort of brake as the car traveled down the road. The study also showed that the airflow over the upper body of the car was largely unaffected by this turbulence.

Supercomputers are able to help create more products than just large-sized machinery. Supercomputer-assisted design systems also aid the creation of molecular-sized products. Pharmaceutical company

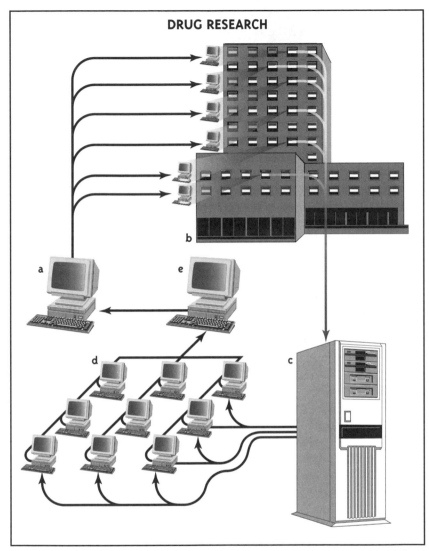

DRUG RESEARCH

Using grid computing, drug researchers can load data from their workstation (a) to their local grid (b). If the task is too big, an Internet server (c) will send it to other computers (d), which will send the results back to the research group (e) and the original researcher.

researchers have been using supercomputers for years to create new medicines and improve existing drugs. Developing medical drugs has been, and still is, a hit-or-miss process of analyzing samples of plants, minerals, fungi, and bacteria in hopes of finding compounds that could combat disease. In fact, some of the world's great pharmaceutical discoveries have come about by accident. Sir Alexander Fleming, a British bacteriologist, discovered the antibiotic penicillin in 1928 when a sample of bacteria he was studying became contaminated with mold spores. He only examined the mold, *Penicillium notatum*, after noticing a large bacteria-free patch around the spot where the spores had landed.

It took more than 10 years for other researchers to develop a way to produce mass quantities of the drug, and even longer to create *semisynthetic* forms of the drug that the body absorbed more rapidly or that counteracted some disease microbes that developed resistance to the original penicillin. Drug companies and academic researchers developed different types of antibiotics by gathering microbes and running them through a series of tests to determine if they had any germ-fighting abilities. These tests included growing the microbes in laboratories, breaking them down into possible disease-fighting components, and testing them on colonies of bacteria and on animals. Similar tests that separate usable medicines from false leads have played a role in the creation of nearly every drug on the market.

The problem is that for each chemical compound that becomes a drug, hundreds or thousands of others prove to be unusable. Fortunately for today's pharmaceutical firms, researchers know enough about how drugs work to create realistic simulations of their activity. Many drugs destroy microbes by breaking through the tough cell walls that protect them from the immune system; others prevent new generations of microbes from forming these walls, leaving them vulnerable to the body's own disease-fighting cells. Then there are drugs that reduce pain, counteract some mental problems, or replace hormones or other chemicals that the body stops making on its own. Each drug has its own chemical mechanism for interacting with microbes or with the structures of the body, and each of these mechanisms can be simulated on supercomputers.

Pharmaceutical researchers run thousands of digitized chemical compounds through specially programmed supercomputers to identify those that could be developed as drugs. By comparing these compounds to previously successful drugs, and to the physical and chemical structures of the microbes or body cells being targeted, the supercomputers can eliminate all but the most likely candidates from any further research. As a result, researchers do not have to spend time in the laboratory conducting fruitless investigations. Instead, they can focus on chemicals that have the greatest probability of becoming marketable medicines.

14

NEW TOOLS FOR THE ENTERTAINMENT INDUSTRY

Though computers were invented for serious tasks, they have become as big a presence in the entertainment industry as they are in the realms of science and engineering. Computer-generated special effects appeared in movies in the 1960s and on television a decade later. The latest home video game consoles are little more than supercharged microcomputers that have been designed specifically for recreation. Game computers and personal computers both incorporate the same or similar high-speed CPUs, digital videodisk (DVD) drives, modems, and other components. Make just a few changes to their circuitry and add a keyboard, and toys such as the Microsoft XBox, the Sony PlayStation 2, or the Nintendo Game Cube would become the equal of any low- or medium-priced desktop system on the market.

Supercomputers have been a part of this high-tech entertainment world for decades. Moviemakers began using supercomputers—leased, purchased, or borrowed—to create special effects at the beginning of the 1980s. Long before then, though, supercomputers had been the subjects of movies, books, and television shows, either as part of the equipment that runs in the background or as important characters in the plot. These days, a feature-length movie can come to life entirely within the circuitry of a supercomputer that has more raw processing power than the dozen most powerful machines of less than 20 years ago.

Supercomputers also are finding a place in the world of digital game playing. Shortly after the turn of the millennium, a number of online gaming companies were considering ways to harness the power of supercomputers to develop and run interactive realms on the World Wide Web. Just as a series of academic and governmental computer networks eventually grew into the Internet and the Web, supercomputers may become the tools of tomorrow's entertainment.

Supercomputers on the Screen and behind the Scenes

It was a little more than four years between the creation of the first supercomputers and the appearance of the first realistic supercomputers in the movies. In 1968 famed science-fiction author Arthur C. Clarke and movie director Stanley Kubrick teamed up to create a wide-screen epic called *2001: A Space Odyssey*, one that followed humanity's development from the dawn of history to the threshold of the universe. The most dramatic scenes of the movie took place in a spaceship that was ferrying a team of explorers in suspended animation to the planet Jupiter, under the supervision of two astronauts. Controlling the ship during its voyage was the HAL 9000, an extraordinarily advanced supercomputer that was able to reason, observe its environment, and even speak with its crew like a human being. As things turned out in the film, HAL also was able to go insane and commit murder like a human being.

In the movie, HAL was described as the most advanced computer in existence as of the year 2001. And while its supposed abilities were far beyond those of any mainframe computers of its time (or ours), HAL was a realistic depiction of the path supercomputing technology might take. Its name supposedly came from "Heuristically programmed ALgorithmic computer," a term devised to suggest a type of problem-solving programming technique HAL used. This term—which combined strictly defined responses to certain situations (algorithms) and general "rules of thumb" on how to apply these responses (heuristics)—stemmed from two areas of *artificial intelligence* research that scientists were exploring in the 1960s. An area of study that developed partly from cybernetics and partly from psychology, artificial intelligence sought to make computers that could think like human beings.

Having HAL malfunction as badly as it did—after declaring during a news interview that it was incapable of harming a human being—continued a tradition of machines turning on their creators that goes back to Mary Shelley's 1818 novel *Frankenstein*. However, while many movies and books featured computers as threats to humanity's existence, others showed computers in a positive and increasingly realistic light. The 1969 book *The Andromeda Strain*, by Michael Crichton, featured an underground infectious-disease laboratory that was controlled by a computer that, while not specifically called a supercomputer, clearly was in that class. And in his 1984 techno-thriller *The Hunt for Red October*, Tom Clancy featured the real-world CRAY-2 supercomputer twice: once in a U.S. Navy control center that analyzed information from an array of sonar surveillance sensors, and once in a U.S. Air Force computing center beneath the Pentagon. In both scenes, the CRAY-2 was the machine that the military relied on to analyze and simulate the sound signature of Soviet submarines.

Cray supercomputers entered the entertainment field for real in 1981, when a special-effects company called Digital Productions leased a CRAY-1S from Control Data Corporation. Digital Productions' founders had produced computer-graphics and other effects for motion pictures and commercials during the 1970s, and they wanted to be the firm that pushed the technological envelope in the next decade. Computer-generated special effects had been simple bits of animation that were composed on regular mainframes, and even some minicomputers. The work that Digital Productions had in mind, though, had never been done before.

Until the 1980s there were two ways to create special effects involving vehicles. One way was to use the real thing—such as a car, an airplane, or a ship—and alter it either in real life or through animation or other techniques on film. The other way was to build a scale model of the vehicle, and then make that model behave as though it was the real thing. This method was the only way moviemakers could create the effects for live-action science fiction movies, especially ones that featured spaceships. Computers had a small role in this work. In the 1977 film *Star Wars* and its sequels *Star Wars Episode V—The Empire Strikes Back* (1980) and *Star Wars Episode VI—Return of the Jedi* (1983), computer-controlled cameras and robot arms gave the illusion of flight to warships, cargo vessels, and interstellar fighters.

Digital Productions and a handful of other companies pioneered a third method. Instead of using computers to give life to special-effects models, the company created the entire effect within its Cray supercomputer. The company's first major project was the 1984 movie *The Last Starfighter*, for which it created such scenes as a flying space car and a heroic battle between a lone spaceship and an enemy fleet. The craft looked sufficiently realistic and three-dimensional on the movie screen, enough so that the effects were one of the movie's biggest selling points. The movie sparked the use of high-quality digital effects in other films, as well as the creation of other computer-graphics special-effects studios.

These days, computer effects are part of virtually every movie genre, not just science fiction. In the 1996 Movie *Twister*, an action-adventure story about the thrill of chasing tornadoes, computer graphics reproduced the power and devastation of these storms. Tornadoes, flying debris, even a cow caught up in the powerful winds were designed and put into motion via computers. In the survival story *Cast Away*, (2000) computer-generated ocean waves turned a small hill in southern California into the coast of a forlorn tropical island. And in the World War II drama *Pearl Harbor*, (2001) computer-generated airplanes, ships, buildings, and bombs took part in a reenactment of the Japanese attack on a U.S. naval base. In each of these movies, and in many more, the computers that created the effects were many times more powerful than the Cray machines that Digital Productions used in the early 1980s.

Pixels, Camera, Action!

A few years before the release of *Pearl Harbor*, supercomputers had become much more than supplements to actors, sets, and cameras. Pixar Animation Studios, the company that created the 1995 film *Toy Story*, and its 1999 sequel, *Toy Story 2*, entirely replaced traditional animation tools with graphics machines to tell the tale of the secret lives of a young boy's playthings. The graphic artists at Pixar assembled everything in the movie, aside from the actors' voices and the musical score, with the aid of 300 computers made by Sun Microsystems and linked together into a single calculating unit. According to one estimate, each of the computers was as powerful as the original CRAY-1.

Short computer-graphics movies—produced on high-speed mainframes or on smaller computers—had been around for decades. Some of these films recreated traditional animation techniques on computers; others went beyond these limits, incorporating extremely detailed effects. But Pixar, which had produced some award-winning short films, became the first production company to create a full-length feature film this way. The big attraction to the film's financial backers was its production budget. Even with the use of complex supercomputers, the movie cost little more than $30 million to make, about one-third of the cost of a traditionally animated movie.

After all, the computer-generated film did not require an army of artists to paint *cels*, the thousands of copies of each character that, when photographed in sequence, give the illusion of motion. Nor did the film require the thousands of clear plastic sheets on which the characters were painted, or the background pictures on which the cells were placed before being photographed. In fact, *Toy Story* did not even require even basic photography equipment, as the movie existed solely in Pixar's computers until the end of its production, when a special printer transferred the final product to film.

For all the savings on human labor and plastic sheets, though, movies such as *Toy Story* place some very difficult technical demands on their creators. Computer graphics are made up of sharp edges and lines. Even when created by advanced graphics supercomputers, objects that seem smooth and round are made up of differently shaded color blocks called *pixels*. Computer graphics artists use a range of programming techniques to smooth out the rough edges and create the illusion of curved surfaces. To make the job of drawing, or *rendering*, the images easier, artists begin creating computer graphics by assembling *wireframe models* of the scenes and objects they wish to construct. (These models get their name because, while they are computer images, they look like something that has been created by bending a bunch of wires into shape.)

A wireframe model is the skeleton of the eventual object; it shows the image's basic structure, along with any other lines or curves that will provide added detail once the model is colored in. Once the wireframe model is complete, the artist fills in the structure with colors, textures, shading effects, and other details to make the object seem more realistic. Computer animators use the wireframe models to position characters within each scene; to program movements, from walking to speaking; and to correct mistakes in the display. Gaps in the surface of an environment's background image, portions of an object that seem to break off when the object moves, lines or panels that seem to fly out from an object's side—these and other problems can pop up when each part of a wireframe model does not match up exactly or when unneeded lines are added accidentally.

Creating a motion picture out of computer-graphic images involves multitudes of computation and coordination. It takes the resources of a supercomputer to carry out the millions of calculations involved in giving life to these electronic puppets and to store completed scenes until the movie is done. Unlike a cartoon character, which is a series of individual ink-and-paint pictures, a computer-graphics character is a colony of digital elements: skin texture files, clothing files, eye files, even hair or fur files. These elements can contain hundreds or thousands of separate details of their own—such as each strand of fur on an animal's body, each of which might move on its own as the character moved—to provide realistic effects.

Even with a supercomputer to perform and keep track of all the heavy work, things sometimes go wrong. For example, while working on the 2001 DreamWorks Pictures movie *Shrek*, a graphics artist mistyped some instructions for rendering the hair on a donkey character (named "Donkey"). All through the night, the computer calculated the position, length, and movement of each hair on the character as it moved through a scene. And when the artist played the scene the next morning, there it was: a walking, talking, donkey-shaped blob of fur. Naturally, the next step was to rerun the calculations for the scene using the correct hair length. As far as mistakes go, this one was easy to correct, but it proved that an old saying about computers held true for the most advanced machines: They can only do what they are told to do.

The Games We Play with Computers

Video games have been around since the early 1960s, the days of the transistor-based second-generation computers. The first truly popular computer game was Computer Space, a four-kilobyte program that featured two spaceships battling each other around a star in the center of a circular monitor. It was the creation of four students at the Massachusetts Institute of Technology who wrote the game on a Digital Equipment Corporation PDP-1, a $125,000 computer designed for scientific use (though not for the same applications as Seymour Cray's CDC 6600). The game became a college phenomenon that students passed from campus to campus over the next 10 years. Computer Space also became the first commercial video arcade game in the early 1970s, when Nolan Bushnell, a graduate of the University of Utah's computer science program, adapted it for a computer that could fit inside a free-standing console. That game did not catch on, but Bushnell's next attempt—a digital tennis game called Pong—was a major success that set off the world's video game industry.

Supercomputers probably did not play much, if any, role in the creation of commercial video games. If they did, the contribution would have been in the form of late-night fiddling around by college students or professors eager to experiment with a high-powered machine. Actually, supercomputers would not have been the right machines for the job. In addition to being too expensive for the first few game manufacturers to afford, supercomputers were too powerful for the task. Most of the time, they would have sat idle, costing more in maintenance than their owners would have earned in sales.

But things changed dramatically in the 30 years or so after Pong hit the arcades, as computers and video games became more powerful and more highly detailed. The technological boom of the 1990s created an amazing amount of growth in the number of computer users and the way they used their computers. E-mail and the World Wide Web drew millions of users on-line. Rapid advances in microprocessor design and other computer technologies produced workstations and PCs that were more powerful than the supercomputers of previous decades. Video games became far more detailed and provided a far higher level of interaction, with environments that allowed characters to move about a three-dimensional environment.

These three elements came together in the middle of the decade. Online gaming—in which players could connect to a central computer using a modem built into their computer or video game console—had been available in a few cities for a decade or so. The new technology allowed an explosion both in the number of people who could take part in a game at one time and in the types of games they could play. Rather than a handful of friends taking part in low-resolution arcade games, hundreds began joining sites on the Web that featured digitized worlds in which the players could become any character they desired. Arcade games—combat games, racing games, and so forth—still existed on-line, but with far more detail and a greater range of playing options than before.

By the early 2000s the memberships of the most popular extended gaming sites ranged from 400,000 to 4 million, providing a serious challenge to the industry. The companies that ran these hugely popular sites—which became known as *massively multi-player on-line games*—had to split the load of the game environment among clusters of computers, each of which contained a section of the game or managed a portion of the players logged on at any one time. Dividing the games this way allowed tens of thousands of people to play at one time, but it caused a huge number of problems. Games slowed during heavy-use hours, improvements or corrections to the game took hours, and the loss of one computer could shut down the entire game site.

Clearly, some people in the on-line gaming industry realized, a supercomputer could help matters. These on-line gaming worlds were nothing more than highly detailed programs that told computers how to process massive amounts of data—something supercomputers were designed to do. Better still, there was a great financial benefit to using a reliable supercomputer. The video game industry as a whole earned more than $9 billion in 2001, and while on-line games earned less than $300 million of that total, industry experts in 2002 were estimating that this figure might grow to nearly $3 billion by the middle of the decade.

Unfortunately, there was an equally great financial hurdle to using supercomputers. A midrange supercomputer costs tens of millions of dollars to buy or lease, not to mention the cost of operating one full time. Despite the possibility of great financial rewards, no one in the gaming industry wanted to take on the cost of such an upgrade. Until, that is, a few companies came along with a less expensive plan to supercharge on-line gaming. The solution these companies—two of which were Butterfly.net and Super Computer, Inc.—offered was a different type of supercomputer, one that did not contain the most advanced technology in a single package.

Instead, their systems divided the huge calculating tasks of on-line gaming into smaller portions that could be divided evenly among a gaming company's existing servers. Rather than having each server working on just one portion of the game, all the servers would contribute an equal portion of processing time to the entire game. Distributing the work in this fashion would make it easier to update a game and fix problems in the system while avoiding the slowdowns and blocks in service that game players hated. Better still, the cost of setting up this system would be measured in thousands of dollars, rather than millions.

SUPERCOMPUTING ACROSS THE INTERNET

L ong-distance computing dates back at least as far as the SAGE early-warning system of the 1950s, which piped information on airplane traffic from radar stations straight into huge mainframe computers. The idea of distributed computing, which allows computers to share data and resources, is almost as old. Government and university researchers around the world began work on this type of computing system—work that would lead to the modern Internet—in the early 1960s. Until the start of the 1970s, though, the only way to use a computer off site was with a terminal set up to communicate with that particular computer.

As mentioned in Chapter 11, the project that most directly contributed to the current Internet was ARPANET, the Advanced Project Research Agency Network. The project's goal was to create a system that allowed scientists to share computer data regardless of which computer they used, and thus speed up work on other projects that ARPA was sponsoring. Other researchers around the world were experimenting with various forms of computer-to-computer communication as well, including experimental radio-based networks developed at universities in Hawaii and California. The ARPANET project, though, created standards for hardware and software design that formed the core structure of the Internet. (A story got started later on that ARPANET had been designed to provide a computing and communication system capable of functioning after a possible nuclear strike. Even though the researchers who designed ARPANET said this story was untrue, it became part of the mythology of the Internet.)

Beyond sharing information, many researchers wanted to connect machines in massive calculating networks, making huge computing engines that could handle calculating tasks beyond the abilities of any single supercomputer or even groups of supercomputers. Networks of linked supercomputers could meet this goal, and major supercomputer centers have been working on putting such networks together. On the Internet, however, a reliable communications network made up of phone lines, satellite links, and other transmission gear already links millions of less powerful computers. With the assistance of *routers*, specialized computers that direct digital traffic throughout the system, Internet users exchange digital information no matter where they are. With all the elements of this global information interchange in place, it was simply a matter of time before someone would try combining the power of the Internet-connected microprocessors into a continent-spanning, or even global, supercomputing superengine.

An Early "Killer App" for Supercomputers

People create machines to make life easier. Rather than carry buckets to and from the Nile to irrigate their crops, ancient Egyptians created a type of simple crane that their modern-day descendants still use to lift water from the river. A farmer can spend days of exhausting effort tilling fields with a plow and a mule; when tractors came along, the job turned into a few hours of driving. People wanted the ability to get in touch with each other without having to track down a public telephone; this is one reason why cell phones caught on in the last two decades of the 20th century. In every case, these tools and machines succeeded because they served a function that people decided was too good to pass up.

In computer terms, functions that are too good to pass up are known as *killer applications*, or "killer apps." Killer apps mostly have been advances in software, the computer *programs* that contain the instructions on how to solve problems, analyze data, and store information. An "application" is a program or a group of programs that focus on a single task, such as accounting or word processing. These two types of applications, in fact, were responsible for an earlier boom in personal computer (PC) sales during the late 1970s and early 1980s. PCs—or microcomputers, as they also were known—had been around since 1974, when an electronics firm called Micro Instrumentation Telemetry Systems (MITS) developed a small, microprocessor-based, build-it-yourself computer kit called the Altair 8800. Announced to the world in the January 1975 issue of *Popular Electronics* magazine, the Altair 8800 attracted the attention of hundreds of computer hobbyists, many of whom were inspired to start their own computer companies.

Within a year, the personal computer industry was up and running—though it mostly was running to find enough customers to stay in business. The problem was that nobody could figure out how people were supposed to use these new personal computers. Few people knew how to program, and fewer people were writing computer programs that were of interest to anyone except other computer programmers. Also, these early personal computers had about as much power as a moderately priced calculator does today, with memory sizes measured according to how many hundreds of bytes they could hold. (The first Apple II computer, for example, held a then-amazing four kilobytes, or 4K, of memory.) There just did not seem to be that much for a personal computer to do, and no reason why someone should pay a couple of thousand dollars to own one.

Three applications turned the industry around starting in the late 1970s. First were spreadsheet programs, accounting tools that corporations use to analyze sales and plan for future business growth. Next came word processors that, at the very least, saved people from having to retype entire pages to correct a single error. Finally, database software provided a means to search a collection of information for a particular group of items, such as organizing a list of customers' addresses according to cities or zip codes. These three "killer apps" immediately made desktop computers attractive to a wider range of customers and opened up the market for professionally produced software.

Just as business-oriented software was the killer app of desktop computing, *e-mail* was the killer app of the public Internet. Sending electronic messages gave people the ability to send messages faster than the post office could deliver them without the risk of playing "phone tag" with repeated answering-machine messages. E-mail also was cheaper and more easily read than a letter sent over a fax machine. As the Internet slowly formed during the 1970s and 1980s—with groups of universities and corporations setting up their own ARPANET-style networks that later linked into the ARPA system—people went on-line mainly to send electronic messages to each other. By the early 1990s the majority of traffic on the Internet came from e-mail; other data files would not begin taking up on-line space until a couple of years later, when the World Wide Web and Web browsers gave users the tools to track down information and images quickly.

Once the data-sharing abilities of the Internet caught up with the abilities of the Net's potential users, the number of people who went online climbed dramatically, as did the number of computers. Unfortunately, neither the phone lines of the time nor many of the computers that served as hosts for the Internet were designed to handle the soaring load of digital transactions that began to flood their circuitry. Servers in particular had trouble processing all the service requests that came in from their routers. Even though the Internet connected computers of all sizes and capabilities, the rapidly increasing number of users began to overload the regular mainframes and minicomputers that made up the system. Entire *nodes* of the Internet would freeze up, locking out any user until technicians cleared the digital logjam (usually by restarting the computers). Throughout the next decade, *crashes* of overloaded Internet servers were a constant obstacle in the path of on-line computing.

The backbone of the Internet, and many of the branches leading to and from it, needed computers that could process thousands of service requests simultaneously. In short, the Internet needed the power of supercomputers—but not the most up-to-date supercomputers available, of course. By the start of the big Internet boom of the early 1990s, $100,000 or less could buy the same level of performance a multimillion-dollar supercomputer provided a decade before. Advances in microprocessor design, combined with circuit-building techniques that came, in part, from supercomputer design, made the increase in speed and decrease in price possible. While top-of-the-line computers continued to handle advanced science and engineering calculations—the original "killer app" they had been created to handle—the slower machines began crunching the numbers necessary to keep the Internet traffic flowing smoothly.

Even so, supercomputer-level processing units have not been the ultimate solution to the problems of the Internet. Crashes and other interruptions still take place, unfortunately, and the ever-increasing number of people going on-line continues to create gridlock. Despite the use of high-bandwidth connections such as a *cable modem* or a *dig-*

ital subscriber line (DSL), which provide faster communication between a user's desktop and his or her *Internet service provider* (ISP), the system as a whole can slow down to a digital crawl. Despite these drawbacks, however, the power of the Internet continues to grow, and if some researchers are successful in their work, the Net may become more powerful still.

Tapping into a World of Resources

In their attempt to adapt supercomputers to the world of on-line game playing, companies such as Butterfly.net and Super Computer, Inc., are continuing a trend that began in the earliest days of public on-line computing. Some of the first commercial computer network services started out in the 1970s as a way for people to link their home video game consoles together through the phone lines. By attaching a modem unit to a console's game slot, a player could dial up a computer and start a game with anyone else. There were limits to these systems—they only worked in a few cities at first, and people generally could play only against others in the same city—but they began providing other services as personal computers became more popular and more people signed up.

Around the same time, dial-in computer services called bulletin board systems (BBS, for short) began offering such features as message exchanges and news reports. In the days before the public Internet boom, a BBS was the only form of on-line computing available to most people outside of the business or academic worlds. Like the systems that turned video game consoles into electronic areas, a BBS gave people the ability to connect to other computers outside their homes. When the Internet became accessible to the public, many users' first Internet experiences came through their BBS.

In many ways, the networks that linked supercomputers in the 1980s and early 1990s were like the old BBS services. They worked either through specially constructed phone lines or through restricted-access telephone numbers that users had to dial directly from their computers to a central coordinating server. Unlike with a BBS or a modern website, researchers could not simply log into a supercomputer network and start calculating. Setting up a connected supercomputing session took time, both to reserve space on each computer and

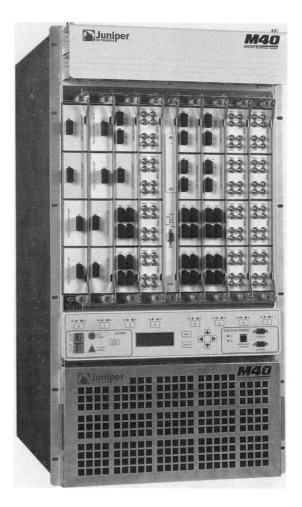

In the past, Internet routers such as this one might have been considered supercomputers on their own. These days, they connect supercomputers and less powerful machines to create the Internet and supercomputing grids.
[Courtesy Juniper Networks]

to ensure that data would be transferred reliably from one supercomputer to another. This method worked well for institutions that could afford both the time and the money to conduct research this way, but many researchers could not take advantage of such a system, if only because there were few supercomputers to go around.

Then, in the late 1990s, computer scientists decided to work on an alternative method of supercomputing, one that harnessed the power of the Internet in a new way. Even the most heavily used computer has moments of idle time, during which the CPU is waiting for tasks to accomplish. People simply cannot work faster than a computer can, and anytime a user pauses or steps away from his or her work, he or she

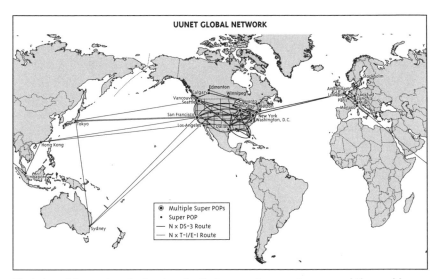

The Internet is a network of networks that connect computers around the world. This diagram shows part of one network, the UUNET Global Network, that comprises the Internet. "UU" stands for "Unix-to-Unix," as the network was created for communication between computers using the Unix programming language.

increases the amount of time that the computer is inactive. Why not, some computer experts wondered, find a way to exploit this unused processing time? Only instead of tying all these processors together to work on one step of a problem, the idea was to split up a problem into many smaller steps and send them around to a legion of computers. The NSF-funded National MetaCenter, the TeraGrid, and the National Technology Grid all proved that it was possible to link supercomputers together in a similar fashion. Gaining access to idle microprocessors, the researchers thought, would simply be a matter of writing the right type of software.

Grid computing—the name given to this type of long-distance computer linkup—taps into this unexploited processing power by using the Internet to do what the Internet does best: transfer huge amounts of information, one small piece at a time. The core of a grid computing system is a data analysis program that runs without interfering with any other application in a user's computer. Once a user installs the program, which might evaluate data on gene sequences or weather systems, the computer downloads a small set of data, processes it, and sends the results back to the institution that is running the project. As more computer users set up their computers to take part in such

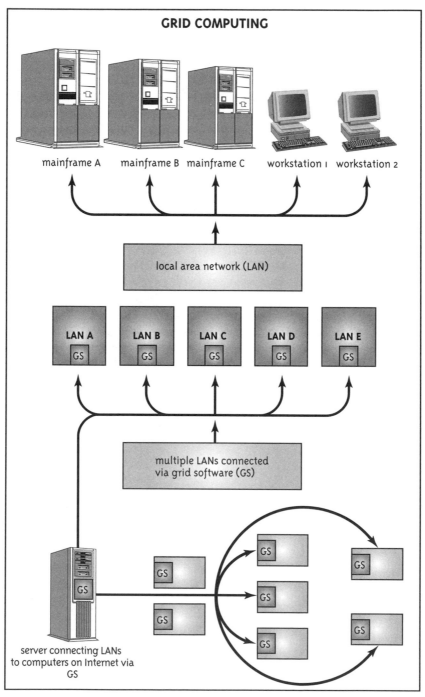

GRID COMPUTING

mainframe A   mainframe B   mainframe C   workstation 1   workstation 2

local area network (LAN)

LAN A   LAN B   LAN C   LAN D   LAN E
GS   GS   GS   GS   GS

multiple LANs connected
via grid software (GS)

GS

GS   GS   GS

GS   GS   GS

server connecting LANs
to computers on Internet via
GS

Grid computing creates supercomputers by connecting computers through networks ranging from local area networks to the Internet.

projects, great amounts of data can be processed at one time, and the overall speed of the number crunching can equal or exceed the performance of even the largest supercomputers.

A Million Steps at the Same Time

Grid computing was still a developing technology at the beginning of 2003, but even so, the idea behind this system of number crunching already had proven itself. In 2001 and 2002, for example, the power of thousands of privately owned computers helped speed up more than a few scientific studies, including the search for new drugs to combat a bacterium that appeared as a possible weapon of terrorists.

Finding new drugs often is a matter of sifting through hundreds or thousands of chemicals to find a few compounds that might be turned into antibiotics, decongestants, or other medicines. Much of this research involves breaking down plants, minerals, and other materials and analyzing their chemical makeup. Drug researchers put the best candidates through further stages of evaluation—including tests on samples of disease microbes and comparisons to known pharmaceuticals—before deciding which ones will make the most effective drugs. Researchers for pharmaceutical companies also take into account how much it would cost to develop a drug and how much of a profit its sale would bring in.

Using computers has cut down the time it takes researchers to sift through and analyze possible drug compounds. The problem is that many potential drugs are overlooked, even when a drug company or a university lab is able to check out each chemical combination. Also, computers that are powerful enough to handle this work are expensive. In the last few years of the 1990s, though, academic researchers developed computer programs that gave regular desktop PCs the ability to sift though possible drug compounds. All a computer user had to do was to download one of these applications and keep it running while the computer was on. The software automatically retrieved batches of data on possible drugs over the Internet, processed the information while the computer's CPU was idle, and returned the results. Participants provided their computers' spare processing time to pharmaceutical research projects, most of which were conducted by university researchers, as a donation to help benefit other people.

This type of on-line supercomputer substitute already has had a major effect on serious scientific matters. On September 11, 2001, terrorists seized control of four commercial airplanes on the East Coast of the United States. The hijackers flew two of these airplanes to New York City and into the sides of the World Trade Center's Twin Towers, which eventually collapsed from the fires those collisions caused. The terrorists aboard the third airplane flew it into the Pentagon building in Washington, D.C. Passengers on the fourth airplane attacked the group of men who had taken over the controls, crashing the plane into a field in Pennsylvania before it could reach its intended target (believed to have been either the White House or the Capitol building). These attacks killed thousands of people—including the passengers and flight crew on all four airplanes—sent the entire nation into shock, and created a fear that other attacks might follow.

Later that fall, an envelope containing a small amount of the bacterium *Bacillus anthracis* showed up in the mail of Senator Thomas Daschle, who was the highest-ranking member of the U.S. Senate's then-Democratic majority. For the secretary who opened Senator Daschle's mail, the only unusual thing about the letter at first was that it contained a fine power that puffed out everywhere. Unfortunately for the secretary and for others in the office building, the bacteria had been treated both to survive a long time while dried and to spread easily through the air. This treatment was unfortunate because *B. anthracis*, the powder in the envelope, causes anthrax, a potentially lethal illness that kills its victims by infecting the skin, the lungs, or the gastrointestinal tract. In other words, the bacteria had been *weaponized*, converted into a form that troops could use to attack enemy soldiers on the battlefield—or that terrorists could use to attack people in cities.

Other letters containing anthrax spores, apparently sent by the same person, went to the offices of other public figures over the next few weeks. Along the way, some of the powder leaked out of these letters into the post office machinery that sorted the mail and onto other envelopes. Five people, including Daschle's secretary, developed and died from the inhaled form of anthrax, while others came down with milder infections that were treated with antibiotics. It seemed as though the anthrax-infected mail had been designed to follow up on the airplane attacks of September 11, though investigators soon decided that an unrelated person had decided to send the letters. But the letter attack showed how vulnerable the public was to such a simple germ weapon. Although five people died after coming down with anthrax from the contaminated letters, hundreds of others, including post office workers working in the sorting centers that processed the letters, tested positive for exposure to the bacteria.

Treating anthrax is a tricky matter of timing. If physicians diagnose anthrax in its early stages, they can fight it with a selection of antibiotics. In fact, during the anthrax attacks of 2001, more than 30,000 people took the antibiotics ciprofloxacin and doxycycline to head off any possible infections from the contaminated mail. But anthrax in its later stages can kill up to 90 percent of its victims. Even worse, there is a major risk that a *strain*, or subspecies, of the anthrax bacterium could develop resistance to the available antibiotics—or that a properly equipped terrorist group could genetically engineer such a strain. The letter attacks, and the new awareness of the risks of international terrorism, made it obvious to public health officials and medical researchers that the world needed new anti-anthrax drugs.

Finding a better way to treat anthrax meant finding a drug that would keep the bacteria from developing to the stage where it can kill people with its toxins. But finding such a drug meant searching through billions of possible chemical compounds that could attack the bacteria. Even with supercomputer assistance, such work could take years to finish if it was conducted using traditional university or corporate laboratories. To try to reduce as much of the burden as they could, researchers at Oxford University in England set up a Web page where PC owners could download analysis software that ran whenever a computer shifted to screensaver mode. What happened next was "unprecedented," according to one of the researchers. More than 1.4 million people around the world volunteered their computer's spare time to the project, which started on January 22, 2002. In a little less than three and a half weeks, the participants' computers analyzed more than 3.5 billion molecules and eliminated more than 90 percent from the field of possible drugs. Even better, of the remaining 300,000 or so molecules, the computers identified 12,000 that seemed to be particularly good subjects for further research.

Each computer might have analyzed just a few hundred molecules a day when the project was at its peak. The fact that so many people were taking part in the project, though, meant that the project took millions of steps closer to its creators' goal with each hour that passed. Success with this and other examples of grid computing has encouraged further work on this area of computer science, and the technique likely will be a strong presence in the future of supercomputing.

PART 4

Supercomputers in the 21st Century

16

OBSTACLES IN THE PATH OF SUPERCOMPUTER GROWTH

One hot day in the summer of 1945, a mechanical brain suddenly stopped working. The brain was the Harvard Mark II, the successor to the IBM Automatic Sequence Controlled Calculator (also called the Harvard Mark I) that Howard Aiken had talked IBM into building during World War II. Like the Mark I, the Mark II performed its calculations using electromechanical relay switches that opened and closed physically as the machine processed information. Though noisy and slow (compared to ENIAC's vacuum tubes), the relays were durable and reliable, so having them seize up for no reason was alarming.

The Mark II's operating crew went hunting for the cause of the failure, checking each relay and each wire, looking for the component that had halted the work of the multiton machine. What they found was a bug in the system—literally. Inside relay No. 70, one of the technicians found the remains of a moth that had been crawling around the Mark II's innards and had been crushed to death. Carefully, the technician removed the moth with a pair of tweezers and taped it in a logbook that the crew used to record all of the Mark II's activity. Just then, Aiken entered the room and asked the crew if they were making any numbers. The crew replied that they were *debugging* the computer, an answer they gave him from then on when the computer was not running.

This incident from the early computer age created the concept of the computer bug, though bugs these days are generally problems in software codes, not hardware components (or actual insects). It also was an early example of how tricky it can be to design a computer that operates flawlessly. The design of the Mark II left the machine vulnerable to anything that could keep its circuits from closing, stray insect included: Its operators had to guard against such things as dirt buildup and scraps of paper working their way into the relays. Likewise, vacuum tubes were the major weak spots in first-generation electronic computers. Only one tube had to burn out to shut down an entire computer for hours, while technicians tracked down the problem. Transistors seemed to solve this problem, until Seymour Cray began packing them close enough together for the heat they generated to melt their circuitry. Similar heat problems have been a bane of microprocessor design from the early 1970s to the present day.

Computer scientists constantly have had to overcome obstacles such as these ever since the days of ENIAC and the Bletchley Park code breakers. As computer systems became more advanced, though, the obstacles became more difficult to overcome. The developments that made today's computers possible, such as the ability to pack millions of transistors onto thumbnail-sized silicon chips, introduced computer designers to a whole new array of problems. One of the amazing aspects of modern computing is that these problems have been overcome, and that computer users have become accustomed to having a constant stream of new and improved machines come on the market each year. However, many experts believe that computer technology may soon reach the point where it will not be possible to push the technological boundaries any farther. The future of computers, supercomputers included, will depend on finding alternative methods.

Enforcing Moore's Law

Computers have been increasing in ability and decreasing in size ever since the first British computer manufacturers went into business in the 1940s. The rate of development in the computer industry is so rapid that comparing computers that are separated by more than a few years is like comparing a Model T Ford from 1908 to a modern-day family car. The Model T was a fine vehicle in its day, but there is no way it could come close to performing as well as a 21st-century automobile. In the same way, personal digital assistants—the handheld, touch-screen computers that people use as appointment books and as Web browsers—contained more processing power in the early 2000s than did most full-size desktop computers from the early 1990s. And while the cabinets of mainframes and supercomputers still can take up huge amounts of space, the amount of computing power they contain would have been considered miraculous in the last few decades of the 20th century.

People expect computer companies to keep bringing out more powerful machines every year because they have seen how far advanced today's computers are when compared to those of the past. As mentioned in Chapter 8, Gordon Moore—one of the men who founded Intel Corporation, the world's biggest microprocessor manufacturer—was one of the first people to notice a pattern to these improvements. While looking over the state of the computer industry in the 1960s, Moore saw that computers seemed to double in power roughly every two years. If a computer that represented the state of the art in 1964 were compared to one from 1962, for example, the 1964 computer would handle about twice the amount of work in the same time as the 1962 machine. These improvements were not just the equivalent of connecting two 1962-style machines and putting them to work, but the result of entirely new techniques of computer design using better components.

Moore wrote about this apparently regular rate of development in the 1960s, pointing it out as an odd but interesting aspect of computer technology and speculating what computers would be like if the trend continues. As the years went by, though, the two-year pattern continued to make itself felt, and computer industry experts began referring to Moore's observation as "Moore's Law." In science and engineering, a law is a generally accepted explanation of a physical phenomenon. Moore's Law seemed to state a simple, observable fact, and over the next few decades it became part of the public perception of computing.

Supercomputers followed a slightly slower version of Moore's Law. Only two companies, Control Data Corporation and Cray Research, built supercomputers in the 1960s and most of the 1970s. As a result, it took years longer to double the power of supercomputers than it took for standard mainframes and smaller computers. Even after the field opened up around the beginning of the 1980s, only a handful of manufacturers developed and made the high-end systems at any time. Still, as the decade progressed, the added competition brought supercomputer development closer to the two-year pattern.

At first, speeding up supercomputers meant packing their components into more compact arrays, reducing the length of wires that connected each circuit board to the rest and providing a much shorter electronic pathway within each board. But there was a limit to how tight these components could be packed without overheating. Just as it took time for one or two supercomputer makers to create new machines in the 1970s, it was becoming more difficult for a modern company to make its incredibly fast systems even faster. To make the more capable supercomputers that researchers demanded, designers began building larger systems that linked from dozens to hundreds of processing, memory, and other cabinets into a single computing powerhouse. The Earth Simulator supercomputer in Japan (described in Chapter 9) is one of the most recent and most powerful examples of the self-enclosed networks, but most other modern supercomputers follow similar, though smaller, patterns.

As powerful as today's top supercomputers have become, though, the supercomputers of the future undoubtedly will be more powerful still. The world and the universe alone provide a limitless number of phenomena to study. The day when human-built computers can analyze all of them will be a long time in arriving, if it ever does. For the near future, computer designers will be able to meet the demand by linking up more cabinets, though at some point it will not be possible to increase computer power this way. The preferred method of computer design has been to create smaller components that can do more work in less space. Unfortunately, there is a limit as well to how small these components can shrink as people attempt to keep Moore's Law in force.

The Limits of Miniaturization

When Eckert and Mauchley built ENIAC in the mid-1940s, a binary digit, or "bit," was a wooden frame filled with wires that linked a row of vacuum tubes to each other and to the rest of the computer. A technician needed both hands to hold it, as it was about two feet long and weighed a few pounds. A little more than 10 years later, when Seymour Cray began building the CDC 6600, a "bit" was a circuit-board sandwich that he could hold in one hand. The transistor technology that shrank the size of computer circuits also led to pocket radios and smaller televisions, ushering in the age of electronic miniaturization. When integrated circuits and microprocessors came about, a bit

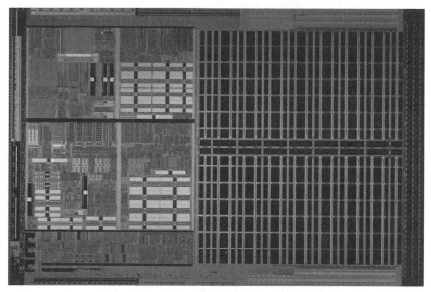

Modern microprocessors, such as this one from Advanced Micro Devices, contain more processing power than some of the earliest supercomputers. [Courtesy Advanced Micro Devices Inc.]

became too small to see: it was no more than a microscopic array of transistors etched on top of a tiny silicon chip.

Since that time, microprocessor designers have devoted their professional efforts to making these miniaturized computer circuits even smaller. Their work has been an ongoing series of successes: For example, microchips that incorporate thousands of transistors and other components are the brains behind such tiny electronic devices as cell phones and digital watches. In turn, the quest for smaller circuits has allowed computer designers to combine the functions of multiple components into one or two microchips, such as creating CPUs with graphics accelerators and additional math processing units attached to the same small slab of silicon. The ability to combine components can both save a lot of space in a computer and reduce the amount of heat it generates. Even a small change such as the addition of sound effects processors to the body of a motherboard can eliminate both the heat and the clutter that a separate audio card would contribute.

The drive to create smaller circuits was not easy. At first, the chip designers' biggest task was to make sure that the microscopic wires and electronic components were distinct and separate from each other. At the extremely small level of detail on these chips, where each wire was only a scant fraction of the thickness of a human hair, it would not be hard to cross-circuit a pathway or two and thus render an entire chip useless. Just a temporary spark across two or more wires or transistors could cause a computer to crash (unless, of course, it simply "fried" the processor altogether). Creating a microchip involves etching the circuits straight onto the chip's silicon surface, using a photographic process that fixes copper and other materials according to a template. After this stage, the circuits are tested using specially designed microprobes that measure low levels of electric current as they travel through the wires. Despite these and other precautions, however, bad chips get through, and even a good chip sometimes has some of its transistors stick open or shut, causing an entire computer to lock up temporarily.

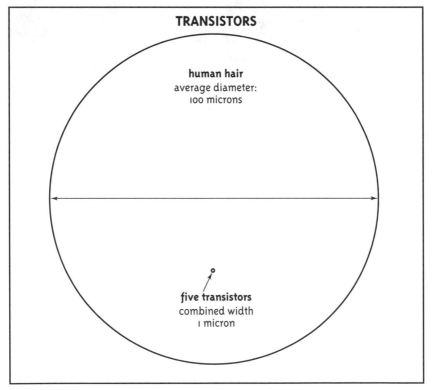

TRANSISTORS

human hair
average diameter:
100 microns

five transistors
combined width
1 micron

This illustration compares the size of a transistor with that of a human hair. Experts predict that the ability to create smaller transistors will end within the first decade or so of the 21st century.

Complicating matters was an old enemy: heat, specifically the heat generated by the computer as it went about its work. As in a toaster or a lightbulb, electricity flowing though a wire generates heat. In some large and small computers, installing one or two fans that force air through the cabinets is enough to carry away the excess heat. High-powered personal-computer CPUs built since the early 1990s, though, have needed special cooling fans to keep their circuits from melting. In the tight spaces of a supercomputer, more drastic measures are needed, as Seymour Cray realized when he refrigerated the CDC 6600. Air conditioning still plays a large role in keeping supercomputers healthy, whether the refrigeration comes from cooling systems inside the computer cabinets or from cooling down the entire space that contains the supercomputer.

Just as these problems were being overcome, another one made itself known. This time, the problem stemmed from miniaturization itself. As the components became smaller, they began reaching points at which they could become vulnerable to the effects of atomic-level physics. Although substances such as metal and silicon seem solid and stable, they actually are sites of intermolecular activity. They stretch and contract in response to heat; they exchange electrons rapidly as current flows through them, or (in resistors such as silicon) serve as dams against the flow. Packing small wires close together raises the chance of having a stray current jump from one circuit to another. The flow of electrons is a powerful force in its own right, a force similar to that of water flowing through a pipe. Just as water can rust or wear down the walls of a metal pipe, electricity can wear out the wires through which it travels, causing the entire microprocessor to fail.

Unfortunately, it did not seem like scientists would be able to overcome these obstacles. Fortunately, they were obstacles that designers would not reach for years to come, and improvements to the technique of building microcircuits seemed to offer an extension of the period that old design methods would still work. Better still, computer designers are, at heart, electrical engineers, and when engineers come up against technological obstacles they cannot overcome, they work around them. The next two chapters will cover some of the techniques that computer researchers have been exploring to work around the problems of miniaturization. But there is another potential obstacle to supercomputer growth to discuss first: the limit on the desire for more powerful machines.

How Much Power Will People Need?

Few, if any, of the people who rely on supercomputers in their work would object to having a computer that was even faster and more powerful than the one they already have. The computer industry makes much of its living from creating and fulfilling the desire for computers that can do more and work harder than those that already are on the market. After a while, though, people begin to ask themselves if it really is worth the expense to buy a computer to replace one that might still be adequate for what they need. This question applies to all levels of computing. Businesses upgrade computer systems only when an old system breaks down or starts to hurt the company's ability to compete with others in the field. Personal computer users generally buy new machines only when they cannot run the latest software or when they want to take advantage of features that the old machines cannot support.

Adding to this situation is the fact that most supercomputers in the world are not paid for by the people who use them. The money for each governmental supercomputer in the world, whether it is used by the military or by a research agency, ultimately comes from that nation's taxpayers. Universities and nonacademic research institutions often get the money for their supercomputers from loans and grants—generally made by government agencies, charitable foundations, and similar institutions—and from partnerships between the university and major corporations that expect to benefit from the knowledge that the supercomputers will help gain. The only supercomputer users who directly pay for their machines, in fact, are the major corporations who use them to research and develop new products and to run the numbers for payroll and other huge accounting tasks.

In all cases, a supercomputer purchase is a committee decision—even in the world of big business, it takes months of meetings and evaluations by company officers to decide if the company needs a new supercomputer and which one to buy. On the other hand, supercomputers are subject to committee revocation, especially when it comes to government purchases. In the United States, Congress has the final word on how much money the government will spend and what programs will get this money each year. For every request for money, there is a risk that someone will decide that the expense is not justified. Even an approved request is no guarantee that a purchase will go through. In the late 1980s and early 1990s, for instance, the U.S. Department of

Energy had begun work on a huge, $8 billion *particle accelerator* called the Superconductor Supercollider, located about 25 miles south of Dallas, Texas. The device, a 54-mile-long tunnel packed with super-conducting magnets and other equipment, was designed as a giant physics laboratory to study subatomic particles at a level of detail that had never been reached before. A few years after construction began, though, the nation entered a recession, a period of economic decline, and politicians began to question the need to spend so much money on a giant atom smasher. Despite the amount of work that already had been done, Congress canceled the project.

Universities and businesses go through similar changes of heart if good times start going bad. Unfortunately, the money from sales of supercomputers pays for research into the next series of improvements, and the demand for these improvements spurs the research. As much as future supercomputer growth will depend on the ability to overcome or work around technological issues, it also will depend on the ability of supercomputer manufacturers to find a market for their wares.

THREE AREAS FOR ADVANCEMENT

What will supercomputer designers do if the day comes when they cannot shrink the size of computer circuits any more? They probably will improve some of the other techniques for speeding up calculations that have appeared over the last few decades. In particular, they may focus on three areas of computer development that already have found their way into modern supercomputing. In each case, these techniques stemmed from the need to push beyond the boundaries of traditional computer architecture.

Until the 1980s most computers followed the EDVAC-based Von Neumann architecture that mathematician John Von Neumann described in the mid-1940s. A single central processing unit performed all the operations needed to work through a computation task, one right after another, in a series of individual steps. This method is called *serial processing*, and it involved a constant exchange of data between the computer's central processing unit and its memory. With the CRAY-2 supercomputer, a second architecture came into play, one with two or four separate processing units that could work on separate portions of a project at the same time. Just as putting more people to work reduces the time it takes to build a house, putting more central processors to work reduces the time it takes to run through a set of calculations. As mentioned in Chapter 9, this method is called parallel processing, because at least two operations or two parts of a single operation are running through the computer together at the same time. Any computer that has more than one processor—two, four, or even hundreds—is considered a parallel processing machine.

Partly in anticipation of the end of miniaturization and partly to increase the performance of existing technology, computer researchers and designers expanded the use of parallel processing through the 1990s and into the 2000s. Some parallel supercomputers combined their multiple central processing units within the body of a single computing system, much as the CRAY X-MP had done. Some researchers even harnessed the idea of parallel processing to give new life to seemingly obsolete desktop computers, using the power of numbers to achieve supercomputer-level performance. All these projects, though, had one feature in common: the application of a concept that came into being hundreds of years before computers existed.

The Importance of Parallel Processing

In the 1790s, Congress wanted to encourage manufacturers in the United States to produce military firearms. At the time, most of the muskets and rifles that America's armed forces used had come from Europe—mainly from France, which was unfortunate, as America was in danger of going to war with that nation. There were many gun makers in the United States, but these craftsmen made their living producing firearms mostly for local citizens and were not set up for large military contracts. Buying from another nation would not be much better. The large gun factories of Europe were simply groups of gunsmiths working together under one roof. All firearms were made by hand, with each gunsmith responsible for building an entire weapon or small groups of weapons at a time. The most a factory could turn out was a few hundred guns each year, and because the guns were handmade, each one was slightly different from the others. This mechanical individuality meant both that each gun performed differently and that repair parts had to be custom made to fit each weapon. During a military campaign, such variations in performance and delays in returning weapons to the battlefield could mean the difference between victory and defeat.

An American teacher and inventor, Eli Whitney, came up with a better, faster way of making firearms and replacement parts that he thought would earn him a government contract to build thousands of weapons. Whitney already had become famous for his timesaving cotton gin, a machine that rapidly separated cotton fiber from the seeds and hulls of the plant. Until Whitney built his mechanism, this task had taken plantation workers and slaves days of hand-cramping labor to finish. Particularly in the South, the time taken up by cotton processing and the delay in getting cotton to market kept the trade moving at a crawl. With the cotton gin, one man could process more than 50 pounds of cotton a day. By itself, the cotton gin revolutionized the industry and revitalized the economy of the South. (It also had the unfortunate effect of reviving slavery, which had been in decline along with the Southern agricultural economy.)

Turning his engineering skills to firearm manufacturing, Whitney proposed the idea of making guns that had interchangeable parts. His gunsmiths would make each piece of a musket—the barrel, the trigger mechanism, the stock—by following a *template*, a physical model of the part or a gauge that ensured each part in a batch was the same shape and size as every other. This method of *mass production* that Whitney devised sped the process of both making and repairing each weapon, as replacement parts would fit perfectly without having to be customized. Whitney's method, which landed him the arms-making contract from Congress, also revolutionized the way factories made merchandise.

The key to Whitney's accomplishment was that his gunsmiths spent their working hours producing just one portion of a weapon. One group of smiths was responsible for barrels, another for triggers, a third for stocks, and so forth. Organizing the smiths this way, rather than having one smith work on one musket at a time, eventually turned the trickle of firearms into a flood, providing more weapons in a shorter time to the American military. Once other manufacturers picked up on Whitney's idea, they discovered they, too, could produce large quantities of goods; better yet, they could produce them fast enough to sell them at prices that more people could afford, yet still make a profit.

Whitney's firearm factory is a direct ancestor of the modern assembly line, in which workers perform the same tasks repeatedly on a continually moving line of goods. In a similar way, parallel processing provides a more efficient method for organizing how computers handle information, with each processor handling different batches of calculations and combining the results into a final answer. Just as the mass-production method got firearms into the hands of American soldiers more quickly, parallel processing analyzes data and delivers the results to researchers more rapidly.

The programs needed to coordinate the operation of multiple processors are more complex than those for single-processor supercomputers. To succeed in rapidly completing its work, each processor has to take up a new batch of instructions or data as soon as it finishes a previous batch. The supercomputer constantly juggles instructions, information, and finished computations, making sure that no processors are sitting idle and that the circuits are not bogged down in electronic gridlock. There always is a slight delay, of course—processing units may have to wait a fraction of a second before an open circuit allows them to send their results elsewhere in the computer or get a new set of data to analyze. But the result always arrives faster than it would have from even the largest single-processor machine.

The first parallel-processing computers were the CRAY-2 and the CRAY X-MP, which were introduced in the first half of the 1980s. The CRAY-2 had two central processing units; the X-MP had up to eight. Less than a decade later, supercomputers had thousands of processors that provided gigaflops of processing power; five years after that, parallel machines had passed the teraflops mark. Along the way, these supercomputers received a new name, *massively parallel computers*, that summed up both the number of processors and the overpowering size of these machines. Nearly all of the supercomputers in the world today use massively parallel architecture to do the work they do. If it becomes impossible to shrink components someday, it still will be possible to increase supercomputer performance by making these massive supercomputers even more massive.

Hypercomputers: All for One

Grid supercomputing, as discussed in Chapter 15, links computers and supercomputers across the Internet into a single computational powerhouse. Essentially a programming technique rather than an advance in hardware, grid supercomputing takes the concept of parallel processing and turns it inside out. Rather than building the machine first and setting up the programs that run it, grid designers created a set of operating software that took advantage of the millions of processors already available on the Internet.

Many companies have gained the equivalent of supercomputer power through a similar system. Instead of using computers in different cities connected through the phone lines, they use desktop personal computers and workstations throughout their office buildings that are connected though a *local area network*, or LAN. LANs link computers to each other, and to *peripherals* such as printers, in an all-inclusive information exchange. LANs can be totally distributed systems, like the Internet, or they can connect the system of computers and peripherals to a central computer, generally a mainframe, that controls the flow of data. Either way, LANS share one other feature with the Internet: unused processor time.

Assume, for example, that a company has a network of 200 personal computers connected to a central server. Each PC can gain access to the files in every other PC, as well as to the files stored in the server's hard drives. However, during the workday, each computer's processors may be idle as much as half of the time, if not more. Even the most productive office worker, who is at his or her desk with only a few breaks, cannot work as fast as a CPU. Tasks such as filing paperwork, answering phone calls, or taking part in business meetings add to the time that people do not use their computers. Effectively, all this noncomputer work means that the company owns a 100-processor parallel computer, formed by each computer's 50-percent-idle time—that is, if the company can harness all the free time of each desktop computer's processors.

With the LAN and the appropriate software, tapping into this unused computing power is simple. Large calculating tasks that are too large for a single computer in the LAN to handle can be broken into smaller pieces, with several processors handling each piece. This networking arrangement of shared processors has the advantage of being able to use any idle processors at any time. The speed with which a problem can be solved depends on how many processors work on it. The larger the number of processors available, the faster the program works out the answer. It almost is like having a parallel processor supercomputer emerge from the computer network that the company already owns.

This kind of network-based parallel computer system is known as a *hypercomputer*, "hyper-" meaning "over" or "beyond," because it enables the computers to work on tasks that would otherwise be beyond their capacity. To make all these CPUs work together on a single task, though, the hypercomputer needs a way to coordinate the tasks that are performed by the processors within the network. The software that distributes these tasks is called a *daemon*, a program that runs continuously in the background while the computer system is running. The daemon has two subprograms, a scheduler and an allocator, that control the flow of work. The scheduler waits for processors in the network to become available, and the allocator sends a message to the scheduler if a process in the network becomes available for use. The daemon also gathers the result of each processor's work and, when the entire task is finished, stores it in the network's central computer.

One of the great advantages to hypercomputing is that, like grid computing, it can be applied to just about any type of computer network. In fact, one of the most notable supercomputer alternatives to appear in recent years, the *cluster computer*, combines features of hypercomputing and grid computing. A cluster connects dozens of ordinary desktop PCs into a single calculating system, with one PC as the cluster's coordinating computer and the rest as computational *nodes*. All the processors are devoted solely to a single processing task, so the system does not have to wait for a chunk of idle time to open up before going to work. And the network that links the computers does not connect to any other network, eliminating the risk of busy phone lines or lost transmissions.

A Beowulf cluster is a supercomputer constructed from hundreds of personal computers or workstations that are linked together and controlled by a sophisticated operating system. [Courtesy National Aeronautics and Space Administration]

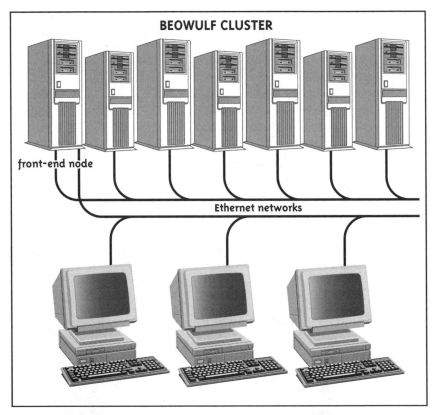

This diagram shows how Beowulf clusters communicate with their users.

The first computer cluster, a system of connected minicomputers created by Digital Equipment Corporation, came out in the mid-1980s. Other computer designers adopted the cluster architecture over the next few years, linking workstations for extra processing power, but it was not until 1994 that anyone tried making a cluster out of off-the-shelf PCs. That year, two scientists at NASA's Goddard Space Flight Center, Thomas Sterling and Donald J. Becker, were searching for an alternative method to get a one-gigaflop supercomputer without having to spend the $1 million such a machine cost. The two scientists designed a PC-based cluster computer that merged the power of 16 Intel 486 microprocessors using an inexpensive Ethernet networking system and a programming language called Linux, which was designed to run on any computer. This cluster was not the one that would stand in for the desired gigaflop machine; the two scientists simply were exploring whether such low-powered computers actually could perform at supercomputer levels.

Even so, it was a critical step into uncharted territory. Just as no one had thought of clustering personal computers before, no one had any idea whether the experimental system would work. In theory, it should have worked just as well as the clusters of minicomputers and workstations that already were in use. Whether the PC cluster could reach the needed processing speed was another question. Sterling and Becker answered that question in 1994. When they switched on their creation, it immediately reached a processing speed of 70 megaflops, only a little bit below the speed of a low-end supercomputer. Getting that level of performance from a bunch of consumer-grade microprocessors—they were Intel 486 chips, the most powerful produced for IBM-compatible PCs before the Pentium series came to market—was amazing enough. Getting that performance for a mere $40,000, which is all that the cluster cost, was all but unbelievable.

Sterling and Becker called their creation the *Beowulf* cluster, naming it for the hero of an ancient English epic poem who single-handedly slew a monster named Grendel (and its mother). When Sterling and Becker announced the success of the Beowulf design, other researchers began developing similar systems, increasing the number of personal computers and eventually reaching true supercomputer speeds. By 2002, Beowulf cluster supercomputers—the name of Sterling and Beckers's creation became the generic term for this type of network—were performing in fields ranging from computer science to geophysics to automobile research and development. They also appeared among the 500 fastest supercomputers in the world, as ranked by the organization Top 500.

Tuple Space: Any Task, Any Time

The third area that may make up for a lack of miniaturization is a matter of software, rather than hardware, improvements, ones that would be of the most benefit to grid computing projects and hypercomputers. With these computers, a difficult problem is broken into smaller pieces, with each piece going to each of several processors. Remember, these processors may be located anywhere, either throughout a corporate network or throughout a region of the world. This is how the networking arrangement of shared processors makes use of idle processor capacity. It almost is like having a parallel-processor-supercomputer genie emerge from an existing computer network.

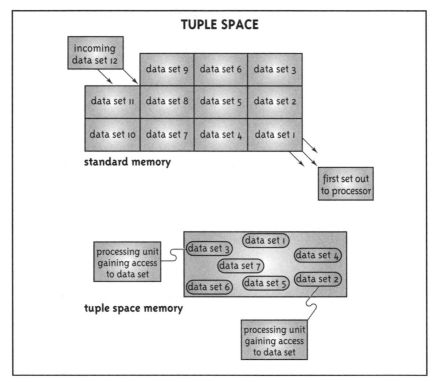

TUPLE SPACE

Tuple space is a kind of shared memory in which data has no fixed address. In effect, computers can access any task in tuple space without regard for its physical location or the order of the items to be processed.

The people who create parallel-processing programs for hypercomputers do not know exactly which processors will run these applications, and they do not know how many processors will be available to run a particular program. To help the program automatically adjust itself for these undefined factors, programmers make use of a concept called *tuple space*.

Tuple space is a kind of shared memory in which the items in the memory have no *address*. "Tuple" means a task or a set of elements; "address" in this case means a bit of data's position within a computer's memory circuits. In effect, using tuple-space processing means that any task can be accessed without regard to its physical location in the computer circuitry or the order of the items. Tuple space holds the input data that has been entered as well as the intermediate results from operations that have already been completed. The speed with which a problem is solved depends only on how many processors are available to work on it;

the larger the number of processors, the faster the program works out the answer. This dynamic freedom of access is compatible with distributed computing systems such as hypercomputer architecture.

In a sense, using tuple space is a return to the concept of time-sharing that got its start in the early 1960s. Time-sharing was a programming technique that allowed a single mainframe computer to handle multiple users at the same time. Even in those days, computers worked faster than the people who used them, and a lot of processing time went to waste when only one person was able to log on. To get the maximum amount of work out of the computer, researchers developed a way for the computer to monitor a series of terminals and to send requests to the central processing unit in the order they arrived. Usually, the people who used time-sharing computers were able to work on their projects without any delays or other indications that there were other people on the system at the same time. Hypercomputing just takes this concept and expands upon it, with the computer taking the extra time from the users.

One of the earliest programming languages for hypercomputing that made use of tuple space was a piece of software called Linda, created by a group of researchers at Yale University. At Sandia National Laboratories in New Mexico, one of the top government-run research facilities in the United States, a group of computer scientists tested the flexibility of the Linda language on a network that connected 13 processors. This experiment, conducted at the beginning of the 1990s, showed that Linda was able to work well enough to compete with a CRAY supercomputer on some problems. Since that time, Linda and other processing languages have helped explore and exploit the computing possibilities of tuple space, enhancing the ability of computers to get every bit of work possible from their circuitry.

18

OPTICAL AND QUANTUM COMPUTING

For all their power and speed, supercomputers operate according to the same principle as desktop computers and digital watches: shuffling electrons through copper mazes to make microscopic transistors switch on and off. Likewise, most progress in supercomputing has come from improvements in conventional computer components, from forcing electrons to shuffle through smaller mazes to writing software that takes advantage of these advances. When designers use nonstandard components in their computers, they generally use components that accomplish the same task as standard parts. Substituting gallium arsenide for silicon in microprocessors, as Seymour Cray did in the CRAY-3 supercomputer in 1984, provided less resistance to the flow of electrons through the chips' transistors. The refrigerating units that still are built into some supercomputers to keep their circuits from overheating serve the same purpose as the well-chilled computer rooms that house many mainframe computers. Even innovative techniques such as grid computing, massively parallel computing, and hypercomputing do the same thing as mainframes and traditional supercomputers: combine multitudes of microprocessors for greater computing power.

The downside to following proven, conventional methods of computing is that supercomputers have the same drawbacks as other computers. For one thing, computers share a similar speed limit. Electrons can flow only so fast through a computer's circuits, and supercomputers contain miles of wiring within and between their components. A lot of time is lost as data wends its way through the copper wire within a supercomputer. Even "big pipeline" connections that convey huge amounts of data between the cabinets of the largest supercomputers only partly compensate for the delay.

Size poses another problem. The average size of a transistor was .18 micron, or .18 millionths of a meter, just after the turn of the millennium. Some of the most advanced microprocessors of 2002 contained tens of millions of transistors in a space the size of a human fingernail. By 2003 some research labs had made transistors as small as .02 micron across, small enough to fit 1 billion onto a typical microprocessor. Compared to the size of molecules and atoms, though, transistors are huge, and it would seem they have plenty of room in which to shrink. In reality, the types of transistors used in traditional microchips will soon reach a point where they will not be able to maintain the separate high-low current levels that allow them to function as on-off switches.

Then there is the question of durability. All electronic components can fail under the stresses of heavy use and high temperatures. Researchers constantly search for cooler, longer-lasting alternatives to currently available components, or at least for ways to increase the lifespan of existing components. Unfortunately, it is difficult to make components that are durable enough to work at the small scale of microprocessors yet are easy to mass produce. Simply put, it soon might not be possible to place more transistors on a microchip. In fact, some computer experts said this point could be reached as early as 2007.

During the last two decades of the 20th century, though, some researchers began working on computing methods that did not rely solely on sending electrons through wires. There are other ways to store and process data than with mechanical or electronic on/off switches. The neurons of the brain do this work all the time by combining naturally generated electrical and chemical signals. Even Tinkertoys, the toy construction kits that contain thin sticks and wheel-shaped connectors, have been used to create a simple processing unit as a college student's class project. For real-world computing alternatives, scientists have explored the possibilities of using everything from individual atoms to living nerve cells. But the two alternatives that seem to offer the most promising results are *optical computing* and *quantum computing*.

Optical Computing

The basic idea behind optical computing—also known as photonics—is to speed up computers by substituting light for electrons. Strange as it may seem, electrons actually are bulky little particles when compared to other denizens of the subatomic world. All physical objects, no matter how small, have *mass*, which is a term physicists use to describe the total amount of matter within things. Subatomic particles such as electrons, protons, and neutrons are tiny bits of matter that carry a negative electrical charge, a positive charge, or no charge whatever. (These particles, in turn, are made up of smaller bits of matter called *quarks*.)

Optical computers use laser light, rather than electrons, to transfer information through their circuitry. In this photo, Dr. Donald Frazier, a NASA researcher, uses a laser beam to create an experimental optical film that could lead to a new type of optical computing component. [Courtesy National Aeronautics and Space Administration [Marshall Space Flight Center]]

The combination of mass and electrical charge causes physical interactions between electrons and the atoms of copper in computer circuitry, generating the heat that circuits give off and slowing the flow of electrons even in the shortest wires. Theoretically, scientists could shrink the wires to the size of just a few copper or aluminum atoms, causing fewer of these interactions. But the greater number of wires this process would allow could end up generating more heat. Heat radiation increases with the increase in surface area, and millions of thin wires would contain such a large amount of surface area that they could turn a microchip into a miniature furnace.

Miniaturization is its own enemy in another way. When components shrink to nearly atom size, they begin to be affected by the quirks of atomic physics. Electrons can jump suddenly from one circuit to another, if the wires of the circuits are close enough together, or circuits can simply stop working. With light, neither mass nor size poses a problem. Light is a form of electromagnetic energy, not matter, that comes in energy packets called *photons*. Like other forms of energy, light can be emitted (as from a lightbulb) and absorbed (for example, by a dark cloth), but otherwise it travels at a constant speed, whether it moves through empty space or through solid glass.

In addition, light can be redirected or absorbed, but no force can alter its characteristics once it is emitted. Because of these advantages, optical processing units could work literally at the speed of light— 186,000 miles per second. Scientists already have created experimental models of computers that use light-based processing and memory circuits. These laboratory models use plenty of standard electronic circuitry in their internal components, as well as in their keyboards, monitors, and other peripherals. However, light-guiding conduits could replace more of these copper circuits in future optical computers.

So, if optical computers are so much better than standard computers, why are there no optical computers on the market right now? After all, some elements of optical computing have been incorporated in computers for more than a decade. Optical storage and recording media such as *compact disks* (CDs) and *digital versatile disks* (DVDs) dramatically increased the amount of data that computer users could store. They also are more stable than magnetic media, such as floppy disks. Laser printers provide both speed and high printing quality, and fiber-optic phone lines have aided digital data traffic as well as clearer long-distance communication.

The problems in achieving full-scale optical computing lie in controlling the flow of optically encoded data and in storing this information.

Electrons naturally flow through copper pathways regardless of the circuits' shape, much as water will flow through a coiled hose if the pressure is high enough. This property makes creating electronic circuits and switches a straightforward matter of design. Light, on the other hand, normally travels only in straight lines unless it reflects off an object or passes through intense gravitational fields, such as those close to a star. For computing tasks, light has to be directed using lenses and mirrors. Even optical fibers, the hair-thin glass or plastic strands that serve as photon pipelines, work by providing a clear, uninterrupted path for light to follow.

Telephone and cable TV companies have been installing fiber-optic cables since the 1980s to take advantage of another property of optical data transmission. Copper wires can carry only a limited number of signals at one time, even when this information is translated into a digital format. Light, though, comes in a nearly infinite number of wavelengths, and optical fibers can carry hundreds of separate signals in each hair-thin strand. Telecommunications companies were eager to take advantage of this ability to provide more services, as it was a simple matter to convert electrical signals to an optical form and back again. But creating the microscopic optical switches that can substitute for electronic transistors has been much more difficult to accomplish. The microscopic mirrors and lenses that would perform the switching tasks would have to be incredibly precise, and such precision is hard to mass produce.

Memory also is an issue. Computer memory chips store applications and data in terms of "on" and "off" transistors. For optical computers, the question is how to capture light-encoded data for the rapid storage and retrieval computers require. It would be possible to convert the light-encoded data into an electronic signal that standard memory chips could handle, at the cost of slowing down the computer's operation. Some researchers have experimented with fiber-optic loops and other types of storage rings that keep the signal traveling in a circle until needed.

The expense of an optical computer system also is a factor. The photons that an optical computer would use are photons of laser light (though *light-emitting diodes*, or LEDs, also could be used in some components). A laser—the word means Light Amplification by Stimulated Emission of Radiation—is a device that creates a beam of coherent light, one in which the photons follow a single wavelength. For optical computing, scientists have been using lasers tuned to emit very narrow beams of laser light at low power levels. But such lasers have to be tuned to very precise wavelengths, and they have to perform reliably at the microscopic level. Achieving this level of precision is pricey. Each optical microchip would need many tiny lasers, receivers, and optical switches in order to work. Researchers have created these types of components in laboratories, but a great deal more work needs to be done to make these parts inexpensive enough to be produced for real-world use. Nevertheless, optical computing could provide the technological solution to Moore's Law that the computing industry might need when electronic miniaturization hits its stop point.

Quantum Computing

Quantum computing is based on the principles of *quantum mechanics*, a branch of physics that deals with the motion of molecules, atoms, and subatomic particles, as well as the way matter emits and absorbs energy. The goal of quantum computing is to make the powerful forces that rule the function of atoms replicate the function of computers.

The theory of quantum mechanics has been around for more than a century. In 1900 Max Planck, a German physicist, was trying to explain the nature of energy. Planck's theory was that energy was not a single, unbroken field of force but a collection of units that he called *particles* or *quanta*. This concept seemed to make sense, given the close relationship between matter and energy. After all, matter emits energy, and matter is a collection of smaller units called atoms. The only difference, Planck thought, was that energy particles existed at different levels of activity, jumping from level to level instantly, with no in-between period. He called this rapid change a *quantum jump* or a quantum leap.

In 1913 the Danish physicist Niels Bohr used quantum mechanics to describe atomic structure using similar terminology. Even in those days, it was clear that electrons, protons, and other particles did not follow the same set of physical rules that applied to larger bits of matter. Electrons, for example, orbited atomic *nuclei* in specific areas, or *shells*, much as a satellite or a space shuttle orbits the Earth. However, it was almost impossible to plot an electron's precise location and its direction of travel within that shell. A researcher could determine either an electron's position at any moment or the direction of its orbit, not both. Also, these atomic particles seemed to make the same quantum leaps from shell to shell that energy particles made from one level of activity to another. These quirks made it difficult to predict the exact interaction of atomic particles with each other, but the overall theory of quantum mechanics seemed to explain the way atoms and subatomic particles behaved.

Quantum mechanics revolutionized physics in the 20th century, but it did not contribute much to the field of computing until 1982. That was when Richard Feynman, a world-renowned, Nobel Prize–winning physicist, suggested that quantum mechanics could form the basis of blazingly fast computers. Feynman suggested making use of another quirk of subatomic particles. According to quantum mechanics, these particles can exist in a number of *energy states,* or points at which they are unlikely to change unless they interact with another particle or force. These states include such features as direction of spin and polarity, which determine the electrical characteristics of the particle. The curious thing is, until someone looks at the particle, it can exist in every energy state at the same time. Just as a researcher could measure either an electron's position or its path of movement, a researcher could identify only one energy state at a time. Stranger still, the act of viewing that one energy state seemed to exclude all others.

Scientists who wanted to run simulations of these and other quantum mechanics puzzles ran into one consistent problem: Calculating all the possible solutions took too much time, as computers explored all the possible outcomes and eliminated those that seemed least likely to occur. Feynman suggested developing a quantum computer that could calculate all the possible outcomes at the same time, canceling out the ones that were incorrect and thus filtering out the correct result. Rather than analyzing data in electronic bits, such a computer would store and analyze data by altering the quantum properties of atoms and subatomic particles, turning them into *quantum bits* of information, or qubits. If a researcher set up a problem correctly and refrained from checking the computer until the end of its run time, the right answer would appear almost as if by magic.

For most of the next decade, quantum computers were considered an interesting, though impractical, idea, as no one thought there could be a practical application for such a computer. This perspective changed in 1994, when Peter W. Schor, a physicist at AT&T Bell Laboratories (which later became Lucent Technologies), devised a mathematical formula showing that a quantum computer could find the prime-number *factors* of large numbers far more quickly than the fastest supercomputers. Prime numbers are numbers that can be divided only by themselves and the number 1. The number 14, for example, can be divided by the numbers 2 and 7, as well as by 14 (14 divided by 14 equals 1) and 1 (14 divided by 1 is

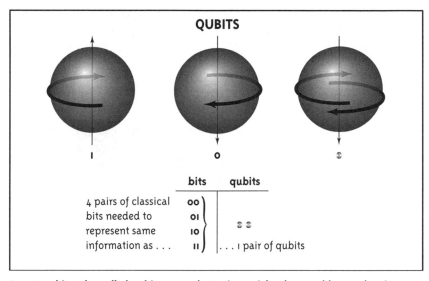

QUBITS

	bits	qubits
4 pairs of classical bits needed to represent same information as . . .	OO OI IO II	. . . I pair of qubits

Quantum bits, also called qubits, are subatomic particles that would store data in quantum computers. Some scientists already have shown that experimental quantum computing devices can perform calculations on the same level as handheld calculators.

14), and thus is not prime. Neither is number 35, which can be divided by 1, 5, 7, and 35. However, the numbers 1, 2, 5, and 7 are all prime numbers; thus, 1, 2, and 7 are prime factors of 14, while 1, 5, and 7 are prime factors of 35.

So, why is all this important to quantum computing? Prime-number factoring is the basis of most high-tech computer data encryption methods. These encryption programs use the prime-number factors of huge numbers—those that are more than 100 digits long—as the key to encode and decode data. Even if someone knew the original number used to create the key, finding the factors using a standard super-computer could take up to 10 billion years. The fact that this task is effectively impossible makes this method so secure.

Schor decided to test whether the security of such an encoding sys-tem would stand up to the computational power of a quantum com-puter. Even though quantum computers existed only as theories on paper, Schor was able to perform this type of analysis by combining high-level mathematics with his knowledge of the theory behind quan-tum computing. For the estimate, Schor decided to have his imagined quantum computer calculate the prime factors of a 250-digit number, the one that would have taken a supercomputer 10 billion years to fac-tor. The quantum computer would need a processing capacity of at least

5,000 qubits to handle the task, Schor decided, given the hundreds of nonprime factors that would need to be tracked down and eliminated.

The result of all this work astounded the computing world. Remember, a supercomputer would take at least two times the age of the Earth to accomplish the task that Schor used as his benchmark. The theoretical time for a quantum computer to do it? About 30 seconds. All of a sudden, the most secure method of encoding data available stopped looking quite so secure. Even though quantum computers were no more than an idea backed up by a selection of academic papers, people involved in security, intelligence, and espionage work realized that there was now a good reason to pursue a real-world version of the technology.

In the decade that followed Schor's work, researchers created a few limited-ability quantum computers. One of the most significant successes took place in 2000, when a group of researchers led by physicist Isaac Chuang created a small quantum calculator at the IBM Almaden Research Center in San Jose, California. The "computer" did not look anything like the handhelds, laptops, desktops, or mainframe computers people are used to. It was a clear tube, roughly the size of a drinking straw, filled with a straw-colored solution that contained a custom-made molecule called pentafluorobutadienyl cyclopentadienyldicarbonyl-iron complex. This jaw-cracker name simply meant that Chuang and his associates had connected five fluorine atoms to a backbone of carbon and other atoms. The fluorine atoms served as the qubits of the computer. The researchers "wrote" data by changing the atom's quantum states using radio waves, and they "read" the results with a device similar to a *magnetic resonance imaging* scanner.

The five-qubit processor molecules gave the vial the computing capacity of an inexpensive handheld calculator—the IBM scientists used it to determine the fastest path through a series of rooms—but it proved that the theory of quantum computing could be turned into a real device. Experts estimated that it would take until about 2020 for quantum computing to be ready to enter the mainstream, as going from the power of a calculator to the power and reliability of a full-fledged computer would take a great deal of time, effort, and money. But compared to the very first electronic computers, whose abilities were not much better than the calculators of today, the early steps into quantum computing are very promising ones.

Chuang's computer also brings up another type of mechanism that has been considered as a possible successor to modern supercomputers. Like the experimental quantum computer, *molecular computers* use specially engineered molecules as the calculating components of ultra-miniaturized computer circuits. The idea that molecules could serve the same function as transistors seemed fantastic, until people realized they already were using a technology that packed tens of millions of transistors on a single microprocessor. Then they were willing to entertain the idea of nanometer-sized switches that—as a writer for the magazine *Discover* pointed out—could store the entire collection of the U.S. Library of Congress in a storage unit the size of a sugar cube.

The molecules in a molecular computer store electric charges in much the same way that core memory did in some of the vacuum-tube computers of the 1950s. Magnetic core memories stored data on round magnets that were mounted on a wire grid. Electrical pulses going through two of the wires altered the field of each magnet, flipping its magnetic poles and effectively switching it "on" or "off." A third wire going through the magnet read its polarity and conveyed this information to the computer's processor. The same principle is at work in a few experimental molecular computers, which use a number of different molecules in place of magnets. The molecules lie at the intersections in a grid of wires that measure only a few atoms across. When low-

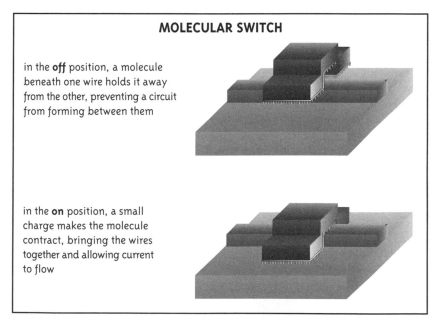

MOLECULAR SWITCH

in the **off** position, a molecule beneath one wire holds it away from the other, preventing a circuit from forming between them

in the **on** position, a small charge makes the molecule contract, bringing the wires together and allowing current to flow

Molecular computers would use molecular interactions at the nanometer scale as part of their calculations.

power electrical currents meet at the intersection of two of these wires, their combined power alters the molecule's electrical resistance, which the grid later can "read back" to the computer. A low electrical resistance, which allows more current to pass through, indicates a molecular switch that is "on"; a high resistance blocks more current, yielding an "off" signal.

As with optical and quantum computers, molecular computers are a technology very much in progress. For instance, while scientists have made working molecular switches in the laboratory, as of mid-2003 they still had not figured out a way to connect these grids to the rest of a computer's circuitry. Experts in the field expect that the problem will take years to answer and years more will pass before molecular circuitry becomes a usable technology. Yet the fact that such fast, tiny components are available, if only for experimental uses, proves that a future of ever-more-amazing computers is possible.

19

SUPERCOMPUTERS ON THE DESKTOP?

By the end of 2002, the quest for speed that Seymour Cray embarked upon in the late 1950s had been going strong for about 40 years. In that time, supercomputers had radically altered how scientists performed experiments, how engineers designed machines, and how people improved the store of human knowledge about the world around them. The computational power of supercomputers had experienced an explosive growth rate that was not likely to stop even if the standards of Moore's Law ceased to apply. Techniques such as linking supercomputers through dedicated networks and combining the microprocessors of millions of computers through the Internet ensured that high-speed computing would continue through and beyond the age of teraflops.

It will be interesting to see what shape these calculating dynamos eventually take. Remember, during the four decades that supercomputer designers were wringing astounding levels of performance from their machines, computers in general went from being huge, exotic mechanical marvels to portable consumer goods that people use to balance family budgets or play video games. In terms of total computing power, the typical home computer of today, which can cost as little as a few hundred dollars, can outperform a million-dollar-plus supercomputer from the early

1980s. They easily dominate the supercomputers of the 1970s, when Cray Research and Control Data Corporation were the only supercomputer manufacturers in business. Even if no other technology emerges to replace microprocessor-based computers—though this is unlikely—computers still will pack more power into a smaller area than they do today.

But what tasks will these future supercomputers perform? Will much of their work be similar to the work they have done so far, or will it involve things that people living at the turn of the century would not consider possible? What follows are just a few of the possible uses for the supercomputers of tomorrow.

Virtual Reality

Virtual reality, or VR, is a shorthand way of referring to a combination of high-speed computers, advanced programming techniques, and interactive devices that are designed to make computer users feel they have stepped into a three-dimensional world constructed of digitized information. Interaction with a virtual reality world takes place in real time, with the user able to manipulate his or her surroundings in much the same way as people play three-dimensional video games. However, a three-dimensional *virtual environment* can be far more complex than the setting of an inner-city car race or a jungle adventure, and many require a level of processing power beyond that of the most advanced game consoles or desktop PCs.

Virtual reality evolved from flight simulators, advanced computer-graphics techniques, and research into innovative ways to aid human interactions with computers. In many virtual reality systems, users wear *head-mounted displays* that create the illusion of three-dimensional vision and *wired gloves* that provide the ability to pick up and move objects using normal hand movements. Other systems use different tools or effectors, such as three-dimensional (3-D) monitors and 3-D mice, to provide this natural interface with the environment. A few systems use entire walls or rooms to create the sense of *immersion* in the digital environment. To be perceived as "real," though, the virtual environment also has to react appropriately to the user's actions and enable the user to ignore the fact that the environment is merely a computer projection. Motion sensors that track user's movements using magnetic fields, inaudible sound waves, or other forms of hardware provide the information that a virtual reality system needs to adjust its performance to the user's actions.

Powerful workstations such as this Octane 2 computer from Silicon Graphics may be the shape of supercomputers to come, with high-speed calculations taking place on a desktop. [Courtesy Silicon Graphics Inc.]

The key to the success of a virtual reality system, though, is its reality simulator, the computer that generates the virtual environment and adjusts it to the user's actions. With the addition of the proper hardware, desktop computers can be adapted to create and maintain simple VR environments, such as the buildings of a centuries-old Spanish plaza or a university campus. (Some computer games come with the appropriate coding to take advantage of this hardware, providing the illusion of depth to flight or combat simulators.) However, as virtual environments become more sophisticated, they require radically higher amounts of processing power to keep in operation. Such high-level computing includes scientific research into global climate modeling and surgical simulation, weapons testing and design, and improvements in virtual environment technology itself.

Supercomputers—though not necessarily the world's most powerful supercomputers—are the only machines so far that have the capacity to create and sustain virtual environments such as these. In fact, a lack of processing power is partly responsible for the spotty history of virtual reality. VR has existed, in one form or another, since the mid-1980s, when separate groups of U.S. Air Force researchers, NASA scientists, and computer programmers created a number of systems for viewing and manipulating 3-D data. (The term "virtual reality" came from Jaron Lanier, a former computer programmer for the video game company Atari who, with a friend, formed his own company to create a more natural computer *interface* than the standard keyboard-and-mouse system.) The concept of a direct interface between computers and users had been present in science fiction for decades. When people learned that such equipment really existed, they eagerly looked forward to the day when they could use it.

Most of these people still are waiting for that day. The first publicly available VR systems, which came out in the late 1980s, cost hundreds of thousands of dollars. Less expensive systems and components came out over the next few years, but the quality of the experiences they pro-

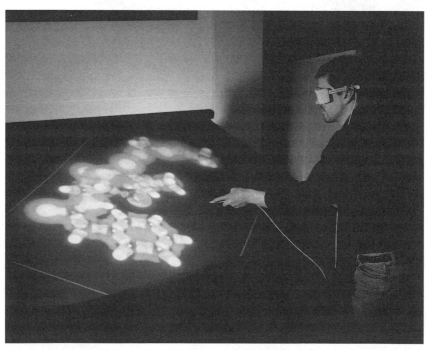

Supercomputers already drive immersive computing displays such as this molecular simulation. Future developments in supercomputing may lead to an increased use of this technology. [Courtesy NASA-Ames Research Center]

vided was far less than people thought they would get. Some of the problems came from the crude nature of these components. The displays that created the illusion of three-dimensional sight were fuzzy, the motion-tracking sensors did not always track motion accurately, and the overall experience often created symptoms similar to those of seasickness. The biggest problem, though, was that virtual environments often lagged behind their users' actions, creating a noticeable delay in the time it took the environment to reflect changes in viewpoint or position.

The computers that served at the reality simulators for the more affordable VR systems were just too slow to perform the seemingly endless number of calculations needed to keep the environment alive. The effect was like trying to download and browse through a graphics-heavy Web site using a dial-up modem rather than a broadband cable or *digital subscriber line* (DSL) connection. Any computer that was fast enough for the task was too expensive for most people to afford.

Widespread enthusiasm for virtual reality died down after the mid-1990s, though it remained a useful tool in fields such as science, engineering, and some types of training, as well as for some video games. With increases in the power of supercomputers and decreases in cost, though, many people in the VR and computer simulation industries believe that the technology could experience a comeback early in the 21st century. Workstations, the $10,000 and higher computers that bridge the gap between desktop microcomputers and mainframes, contained as much processing ability in the early 2000s as some supercomputers from less than a decade before. This capacity made them just powerful enough to perform all the functions of a reality simulator. Because computer abilities increase rapidly, VR experts thought that most people would be able to afford immersive computing systems by the 2010s. If so, these VR systems probably would find a ready market waiting for them—the computer users who are taking part in the on-line game-playing of the Internet.

Artificial Intelligence

For decades, computer researchers have dreamed of creating a computer that can follow instructions, provide answers, and even reason like a human being. Such a computer would need to be able to mimic the brain's ability to learn new information and relate this data to what it already knows, to analyze uncertain or confusing situations and come up with a correct response, and to improve its performance based on these experiences. This type of computing is called artificial intelligence, and it is considered one of the most challenging fields of computer research.

For example, consider that a computer is ordered to perform a simple task like stacking different-sized blocks on a table using a robot arm. To perform this task, the computer first would have to be able to recognize that it has an arm at its disposal; that the square, wooden things on the table were blocks; and that blocks could be placed on top of other blocks. The computer then would have to decide which block would be on the bottom and which ones would form the body of the stack. As the computer worked its way through the task, it would need to be able to learn from discoveries it makes along the way, such as "placing the smallest block on the bottom can make the stack fall over." And once it had successfully finished its work, the computer would have to be able to repeat it without going through a similar process of trial by error.

Artificial intelligence research has focused on a number of areas that reproduce different facets of human thought. The block-stacking task combines two of these areas, *problem solving* and *machine learning*. In problem solving, the computer has to go from a beginning state to a goal in as few steps as possible. Machine learning is the improvement in how a computer handles a task as it analyzes its past performance and applies this knowledge to future attempts. Other areas of artificial intelligence research include *pattern recognition*, in which the computer separates particular objects or types of data from a larger group; *game theory*, in which the computer plays a game by choosing which moves have the best probability of leading to a win; and *natural language processing*, the ability to interpret phrases such as "throw me the ball" as meaning "throw the ball to me" rather than "throw me to the ball."

Of all the fields of computer research, artificial intelligence has been the slowest to achieve results that can be used in the real world. Human beings can learn from experience, win board games, and understand the difference between throwing balls to people and vice versa because of the way their brains work. In addition to being a powerful data-processing engine, the human brain is very flexible, capable of forming new circuits throughout its working life.

Computers, though, generally are inflexible. Once built, they cannot form new circuits on their own, and they are incapable of the intuitive leaps that people make every day. To compensate for this difference, artificial intelligence researchers use combinations of hardware and software techniques that create mathematical rules for reproducing how the brain processes data. These mathematical rules, called *algorithms*, provide a starting point from which computers can calculate appropriate responses to unfamiliar situations.

For all the difficulty in recreating the operation of the human brain, artificial intelligence researchers have developed some amazing techniques. The most successful artificial intelligence project so far has been the creation of *expert systems*, computer programs that provide advice on how to proceed with tasks in a given field. Also called knowledge-based systems, expert systems combine sets of rules for analyzing data with huge databases that contain information about the subject being explored, which can range from medicine to geology. Using an expert system can be as simple as entering data about an unfamiliar phenomenon, answering a series of brief questions about the subject, and having the computer offer an opinion based on its analysis of the data and related information in its database. The rules, or knowledge base, that the system follows to reach its conclusions are designed to reproduce the thought process a human expert in the field would follow if he or she were asked to solve the same problem.

Expert systems do not truly recreate the function of the mind of an expert in chemistry, genetic engineering, or any of the other fields to which the technology has been applied. However, sufficiently powerful computers with great amounts of processing and data storage ability are better at creating the illusion that the system knows what it is talking about. With sufficiently powerful supercomputers and the proper programming, other facets of artificial intelligence could become more sophisticated and realistic themselves. If that happened, and the techniques were adapted for use with powerful home PCs, using a computer might become as simple as discussing a project and asking the machine to fill in the gaps.

Cybernetics

One other aspect of artificial intelligence deserves special mention. *Cybernetics* is the study of how living creatures, including humans, take in and process information, and how this activity compares to that of mechanical and electronic systems. The important issue in cybernetics is how information flows through the system being studied, regardless of what that information contains. It could be a company's annual report, instructions for filing tax returns, or the watering schedule for an automatic sprinkler system. What matters is how the information finds its way to its final destination.

As mentioned in Chapter 3, the field of cybernetics appeared before the creation of the Mark I, ENIAC, and Colossus. These machines, and the first-generation computers that followed them, provided a perfect opportunity to test theories of information processing that could not be duplicated in any other way. Cybernetics and computers were such a good match, in fact, that the word *cybernetics* became associated with computers in the public's mind, and the prefix "cyber-" came to mean anything associated with computing.

In truth, cybernetics involves more than computer design and programming, just as sewing involves more than making shirts and dresses. Cybernetics includes discussions of the most efficient manner in which signals can reach their destination and of how systems decide which signal in a group of signals is given the greatest priority. None of the issues of cybernetics is exclusive to the world of computing, but all of them apply to the refinement of computer programming and architecture. In a future in which supercomputers could reach titanic proportions—in terms of both size and processing abilities—these advanced theories of how systems handle information will provide the techniques for getting the maximum level of performance from the great machines.

Supercomputers may remain the tools of big science and big business, or they may become everyday fixtures in the homes of tomorrow. They may take the form of tabletop boxes or of world-spanning networks of microprocessors. Whatever happens, people will always have a need for the type of work that only supercomputers can do. There will always be a natural phenomenon to examine or an engineering problem to resolve that cannot be handled any other way. As long as people continue to expand the boundaries of knowledge and innovation, supercomputers will be a part of their engine of discovery.

GLOSSARY

absolute zero   The temperature at which molecules stop moving and contain no energy. Absolute zero—also referred to as zero degrees on the Kelvin scale—is equivalent to −273.15 degrees Celsius (273.15 degrees below the freezing point of water) or −459.67 degrees Fahrenheit.

address   In computing, the location of a bit of data within a computer's memory or processing circuitry.

adenosine   One of the three chemical bases present in the nucleotides of both DNA and RNA.

algorithm   A mathematical rule or model for solving problems in a systematic fashion.

amino acid   A chemical compound that serves as a basic building block of protein molecules.

amplitude   A measure of the amount of disturbance created by a wave. The amplitude of a wave on a lake, for example, is the distance between the top (crest) or bottom (trough) of the wave and the surface of the lake when it is calm.

analog   In computing, said of a device that measures a constantly varying equation, such as one representing a change in temperature or speed.

antimatter   Matter that consists of negatively charged nuclei and positively charged electrons. Antimatter is the opposite of matter in our universe, which has positively charged nuclei and negatively charged electrons.

application   In computer terms, the program or set of instructions that directs a computer to carry out a sequence of calculations, store data, or perform other tasks. Word processors and games are types of applications.

artificial intelligence (AI) A field of computer science that seeks to reproduce the function of human analysis and reasoning.

architecture In computer terms, the design of a computer system that determines how a computer processes data.

axis A mathematical term that refers to the three directions of movement in the physical world. The plural of *axis* is *axes* (pronounced "acks-eez"). The three axes are the X (left/right) axis; the Y (up/down) axis; and the Z (forward/back) axis. These three axes also are known as the Cartesian axes.

Bacillus anthracis The bacterium that causes the potentially deadly disease anthrax. This bacterium is one of many that have been WEAPONIZED.

backbone In computing terms, the group of linked computers that forms the central communication structure of a network.

base In genetics, one of the chemicals in DNA and RNA that form genes.

base metal A common metal of little or no economic value.

Beowulf cluster A compilation of ordinary PC-style computers that provides the calculating power of a supercomputer without the construction or maintenance costs.

binary number system The mathematical system in which numbers are written as strings of 0s and 1s. The position of each 0 and 1 within the string determines the value of the number that string represents. The binary system is well suited to computers and is the foundation of all computer languages: An electrical switch that is OFF can represent 0 and a switch that is ON can represent 1. *See* DECIMAL NUMBER SYSTEM.

binocular parallax The brain's ability to perceive three-dimensional depth and distance by combining the slightly offset images sensed by each eye.

black hole An extremely dense collapsed star with a gravitational force so powerful that even light cannot escape its pull.

boson A subatomic particle that controls interactions between matter and carries the four basic forces of nature: gravity, electromagnetism, the "weak" nuclear force that affects some forms of radioactive decay, and the "strong" nuclear force that binds protons and neutrons together in the center of an atom.

bulletin board system (BBS) A modem-based computer system that allows users to exchange messages and download information.

CD-ROM *See* COMPACT DISC-READ ONLY MEMORY.

cable modem A component that connects a computer system to a network, such as the Internet, through the same type of copper or fiber-optic lines that carry television signals.

calculus A branch of mathematics that deals with variable equations, those in which the numerical values of some quantities constantly change.

cathode-ray tube (CRT) A vacuum tube that forms images by shooting electrons from a negatively charged source (a cathode) to a phosphorescent screen that glows when hit by the electrons. Electromagnets inside the vacuum tube bend the beam, forcing it to rapidly scan across the surface of the screen. Color television sets and computer monitors have differently colored screens in the same CRT.

cel In traditional animation, a sheet of clear plastic (originally, cellophane) on which a character or a portion of a character is painted. The illusion of movement comes from photographing thousands of cels against a background.

central processing unit (CPU) The primary collection of circuits within a computer that carries out calculations and acts upon instructions. A CPU can be thought of as the "brains" of the computer.

circuit A pathway for electricity formed by the wires in an electrical device.

circuit board A board in a computer or other electronic device that houses microprocessors or other components connected by printed or etched wire circuits.

cluster computer A network of standard consumer-grade computers (such as desktop PCs) that combines the power of their microprocessors into a single computing engine. Many cluster computers are able to run at supercomputer speeds.

cluster, galactic *See* GALACTIC CLUSTER.

coarse-grained system A computer system that uses a few powerful, full-scale processors.

compact disk (CD) A plastic-covered aluminum disk that contains digital information in the form of small pits etched into the disk's surface by a laser.

compact disk–read only memory (CD-ROM) A compact disk that contains text, audio, and visual computer files that can be read by a computer drive but that cannot be altered.

compiler A computer program that translates instructions written in a symbolic language such as FORTRAN or UNIX, which programmers can understand, into the machine language that computers can act upon.

computer-aided design   The process of using specialized computer software to create the plans for buildings, machines, or other structures.

computer-assisted machinery   Automated machines on an assembly line that are under the control of a computer.

computer graphics   Visual displays created using computers. A simple bar graph created with a word processor technically is an example of computer graphics. However, the term usually refers to more advanced displays such as those in video games or flight simulators.

conductor   In electronics, a material that allows electricity to flow easily. Copper and gold are particularly good conductors of electricity; this is why power cables contain copper wiring and why computer circuits use copper and gold.

crash   In computing terms, a sudden failure of an application, a computer system, or a network.

CRT   *See* CATHODE-RAY TUBE.

cybernetics   The study of how living creatures, including humans, take in and process information, and how this activity compares to that of mechanical and electronic systems.

cyberspace   The virtual world created by the Internet and other computer networks in which people communicate and share information. William Gibson, a science-fiction author, coined the word in his 1983 novel *Neuromancer.*

cytosine   One of the three chemical bases present in the nucleotides of both DNA and RNA.

daemon   In computing terms, a program in a hypercomputer network that distributes and coordinates tasks among the network's processors.

database   A collection of information stored as a computer file that is set up to allow people to easily retrieve that information.

data parallelism   A data-processing technique in which the computer carries out the same operation on many portions of data at the same time. With this method, the computer's speed is determined by the amount of data that needs to be processed, not by the number of steps the computer has to take.

data point   An area where researchers gather information for analysis. Generally, data points are at the intersections of a data-collection grid that is imposed on a community, a section of the sky, or another sampling area.

debugging   The process of eliminating errors or malfunctions in a computer or in a computer program.

decimal number system   The mathematical system in which numbers are written using the digits 0 through 9.

deoxyribonucleic acid (DNA)   One form of genetic material that determines an organism's shape, function, and other characteristics. DNA molecules consist of long sequences of smaller units called nucleotides (*see* NUCLEOTIDE).

desktop computer   In general, any computer that can fit on a desk. *See* PERSONAL COMPUTER.

digital subscriber line (DSL)   A specialized Internet connection technique that uses standard phone lines to transmit high-speed digital data signals.

digital versatile disk (DVD)   A storage disk that is similar to a compact disk but holds more information. DVDs are used to record movies and to store very detailed computer programs and information databases.

effector   In virtual reality computing, any device used to display or control a virtual environment.

electric potential   The ease with which any material conducts electricity. Electric potential is measured in volts.

electromagnetic force   In physics, the combined properties of electricity and magnetism. Electricity and magnetism are very similar forces: every electric current generates a magnetic field, and every magnetic field can be made to generate an electric current. Because electricity and magnetism are so strongly linked, scientists consider them aspects of the same force. Other examples of electromagnetic force are light waves, radio waves, and microwave radiation.

electron   A subatomic particle that carries a negative electromagnetic charge and forms part of the structure of atoms. Electric appliances and electronic devices work by exploiting the flow of electrons through conductive materials such as metal.

electronic mail   *See* E-MAIL.

e-mail   Documents, photographs, messages, and other materials transmitted through the Internet or other computer networks.

energy state   In quantum mechanics, a condition of stability in an atomic or other system.

environment   *See* VIRTUAL ENVIRONMENT.

expert system   A computer program that uses artificial intelligence techniques to analyze problems and offer advice or potential solutions. Also called knowledge-based systems.

factor A number or a quantity that evenly divides a larger number or quantity. The numbers 3 and 15 divide the number 30 without a remainder (30/3=10 and 30/15=2); thus, 3 and 15 are factors of 30. The number 7 divides the number 15 with a remainder (15/7=2.5); therefore, 7 is not a factor of 15.

fermion The group of subatomic particles that includes electrons, protons, and neutrons.

fiber optics The use of optical fibers to transmit information.

fifth-generation computers Computers that contain ultra-large-scale integration (ULSI) processors, with microchips containing from 2 million to 64 million transistors.

fine-grained system A computer system that uses large numbers of less-powerful processors.

first-generation computers Computers whose circuitry used vacuum tubes as switches. First-generation computers also incorporated magnetized metal drums or cathode-ray tubes (similar to television tubes) for memory and punched cards for data input and output. The first generation of computing technology covers the period from 1943 to 1958.

flight simulator A device or computer program that reproduces the effects of airplane or helicopter flight.

fluid dynamics The branch of physics that covers the complex flow of gases and liquids.

fourth-generation computers Computers whose circuitry centered on the use of microprocessors, such as the central processing unit that serves as the core of modern personal computers. The fourth generation of computing technology started in 1971 and is still being used today. Advanced versions of these computers have enough memory capacity to allow the processing of enormous quantities of data and thousands of simultaneous users. Early fourth-generation computers had large-scale integrated (LSI) circuits; current versions incorporate very-large-scale integrated (VLSI) circuits that may contain millions of transistors.

frequency A measurement of how many waves travel through a substance in a given amount of time. For example, humans can hear from as few as 15 to as many as 20,000 sound waves per second.

frontal system The area where air masses of different temperatures or densities come against each other.

functional parallelism A data-processing technique in which the computer operates simultaneously on separate parts of the data needed to solve a problem. Each operation is kept separate until the results are combined to reach an answer.

galactic cluster   A group of closely spaced galaxies held together by the force of gravity.

galaxy   A huge, rotating collection of stars, star systems, gas, and dust that is held together by gravity and the force of its rotation.

game theory   In artificial intelligence, the technique of programming a computer to choose game moves that are most likely to lead to a win.

gene   A sequence of nucleotide bases on a DNA molecule that determines the characteristics of living things.

genome   The complete genetic sequence of a living creature.

gluon   A subatomic particle that carries the strong force that binds quarks together to form larger particles.

grand-challenge problem   A complex research task that involves more than one area of science or engineering.

guanine   One of the three chemical bases present in the nucleotides of both DNA and RNA.

head-mounted display (HMD)   A computer or television monitor that rests on or otherwise attaches to the head of a user. HMDs can incorporate headphones and position trackers, and can provide either a semitransparent view (as in augmented reality) or a fully enclosed display (as with most virtual reality systems).

helix   A spiral shape, similar to the rails of a spiral staircase.

HMD   *See* HEAD-MOUNTED DISPLAY.

hyperchannel   The circuitry that links all the parts of a supercomputer and is the main information carrier.

hypercomputer   A parallel computer system that makes use of idle processors in a network of computers. For example, a company may have a network of workstations that are not used all the time, or whose processors are inactive for much of the time the workstations are being used. With the proper programming techniques, the company can use these idling processors to perform large-scale calculating tasks without interrupting the work each computer user is doing. This way, the company effectively owns a multiprocessor parallel computer.

hypothesis   In science, a possible explanation for a physical phenomenon that must be proved by experimentation.

icon   A small picture used to represent a computer program. When selected, an icon activates the application it represents.

immersion   The sense of being surrounded by a virtual environment.

input/output (I/O)   Input is the data users enter into computers; output is the result of a computer's calculations or a computer user's tasks. I/O is used as a measure of how fast a computer works. Super-computers have extremely high rates of I/O processing.

insulator   A material such as glass, rubber, or plastic that does not allow electricity to pass through itself.

integrated circuit   A complete electrical circuit—including wires, switches, and other components—that has been etched onto a single chip of material such as silicon.

interactive   Capable of conducting command-and-response interactions between users and computers with little or no time lag.

interface   In computer terms, the method by which people use computers.

Internet   A globe-spanning network of interconnected computer systems. Though it is the best-known network, the Internet is actually just one of several networks that exist to help people exchange news and ideas with one another.

Internet service provider (ISP)   A telecommunications company that provides access to the Internet, generally for a fee, through a collection of privately owned servers and routers.

jet stream   A high-speed current of air that blows through the upper atmosphere.

joystick   A post-shaped control device that allows movement in two of the three dimensions. A 3-D joystick allows movement in all three dimensions (forward/back, left/right, up/down).

killer application (killer app)   An extremely popular or useful computer program that creates a high level of demand among potential users.

knowledge-based system   *See* EXPERT SYSTEM.

lag time   The delay between an action and the effects of that action. In virtual reality, lag time reflects how long it takes a virtual environment to catch up to a user's movement.

laser   An optical device that creates a narrow beam of coherent light in which all photons share the same physical characteristics.

LCD   *See* LIQUID-CRYSTAL DISPLAY.

LED   *See* LIGHT-EMITTING DIODE.

lepton   A subatomic particle that is one of the basic building blocks of matter.

light amplification by stimulated emission of radiation   *See* LASER.

light-emitting diode (LED)   A diode is an electronic component that lets current flow in one direction but prevents it from flowing in the other. A light-emitting diode is a diode that produces light as current flows through it. LEDs use very little energy.

liquid crystal A normally transparent liquid material that turns opaque when an electric current runs through it.

liquid-crystal display (LCD) A computer display made up a liquid-crystal material trapped between separate layers of glass or plastic.

local area network (LAN) A computer network that connects a small number of computers and peripherals, generally centered on a single server.

machine language A computer programming language that provides instructions as strings of 1s and 0s (*see* BINARY NUMBER SYSTEM). Because computers perform calculations by rapidly setting switches to "on" and "off" states (actually, high and low levels of electric flow through a circuit), the 1s and 0s represent these "on" and "off" states.

machine learning In artificial intelligence, the ability of a computer to improve its ability to complete a task by learning from prior attempts.

magnetic resonance imaging (MRI) A scanning device that uses powerful magnets and radio waves to scan the interior of a body or another object.

mass The total amount of matter within an object.

massively multiplayer on-line games Role-playing computer games offered on the World Wide Web that host from tens of thousands to millions of users.

massively parallel computers Parallel-processing supercomputers that contain thousands of microprocessors.

mass production A manufacturing technique that divides the construction of an item into a series of steps, each of which is performed by a separate group of workers. This method both speeds up the process of making merchandise and lowers the cost of production.

mechanical tracker A position tracker that uses electronic linkages attached to mechanical joints to measure movement.

memory Circuits in a computer that store instructions and data for use during calculations. In a multiprocessor computer, each processor may have its own memory, share a central memory, or use a combination of both types.

microchip A tiny slice of semiconductive material that forms the base of an integrated circuit; also, another term for a microprocessor.

microcomputer *See* PERSONAL COMPUTER.

microprocessor   A type of integrated circuit that contains a computer's master control circuitry.

minicomputer   A table-sized or cabinet-sized computer that appeared in the early-to-mid-1960s, following the introduction of transistors to computer circuitry.

modem   A device that transforms digital data from a computer into analog form—which can be transmitted over communication lines such as telephone lines—and converts analog data it receives into digital form. The word comes from the term *mo*dulation-*dem*odulation: modulation is the conversion of digital signals to analog form, while demodulation is the conversion of analog signals to digital form.

motion sensor   *See* POSITION TRACKER.

motion tracker   *See* POSITION TRACKER.

mouse   A computer device that uses a rolling ball and at least one button to control an on-screen cursor. A standard computer mouse provides only two-dimensional (up/down and left/right) movement. The plural is *mice*.

mouse, 3-D   A computer mouse used to navigate in three-dimensional computer environments.

nanometer   One-billionth of a meter, roughly 39-billionths (0.000000039) of an inch.

nanosecond   One-billionth of a second.

natural language processing   In artificial intelligence, the ability of a computer to understand the meaning of everyday language, as opposed to sentences that follow strict rules of grammar.

neutron   A subatomic particle that does not carry an electromagnetic charge. A neutron is one of the two particles that can form the nucleus of an atom; the other is the proton.

node   In computing terms, a single processor that is part of a computer-processing network. "Node" also refers to a computer that serves as a component of the Internet or similar network of computers.

nuclei   The plural of NUCLEUS.

nucleotide   The basic structural unit of a DNA or RNA molecule. Each nucleotide consists of a sugar molecule, a phosphate group (a phosphorous atom connected to four oxygen atoms), and a chemical called a base. DNA has four bases, known as adenine (A), cytosine (C), guanine (G), and thymine (T). A sequence of three nucleotide bases along the DNA molecule contains the code for one amino acid.

nucleus   In physics, the central structure of an atom. In biology, the structure in a cell that contains the cell's DNA.

operating clock speed   The smallest period of time in which synchronized operations take place within a computer.

operating program/operating system   The set of instructions that controls and coordinates how a computer system works.

optical computing   The use of light rather than electrons to process and store information in a computer.

optical fiber   A solid, very thin glass or plastic fiber that can transmit light around curves.

output   *See* INPUT/OUTPUT.

parallel processing   The execution of several operations or several parts of an operation on a computer at the same time. In general, the term applies to computers that have more than one processor, especially a very large number of processors.

particle accelerator   A device that uses fast-moving beams of charged subatomic particles, such as electrons, to study the interior structure of atomic nuclei.

pattern recognition   In artificial intelligence, the ability of a computer to separate a particular set of objects or data from a larger mixed group.

Penicillium notatum   The mold that originally yielded the antibiotic penicillin.

peripheral   Any device that connects to a computer. Examples of peripherals include keyboards, mice, monitors, and printers.

perovskites   A class of ceramic materials with a crystalline structure that behave somewhat like a metal. Some perovskites are superconductors at relatively high temperatures.

photon   A pulse of electromagnetic energy that is the basic unit of light.

photonics   *See* OPTICAL COMPUTING.

photoreceptor   A mechanical or electronic device, or a group of cells, that can detect light.

pipelining   A method of parallel processing in which several computer operations—such as preparing data for computation, calculating sums, or storing the results of previous calculations—may take place at the same time.

pixel   From "picture element." A small block of color used to create a computer graphic image.

polarity   The alignment of an electromagnetic force such as light waves. An example is the north-south orientation of a magnetic field.

polarization   The separation of an electromagnetic force into different polarities.

polarizer   Something that can separate polarities.

position tracker   An effector that lets a virtual reality system monitor which way a user moves his or her head, arms, legs, hands, or whole body.

problem solving   In artificial intelligence, the process of going from a starting state to a desired goal in the fewest possible steps.

program   The instructions that tell a computer how to solve a problem, analyze data, or store information.

protocol   In computing terms, a standard programming format that controls how information is transmitted between computers or between components within a computer.

protogalaxy   A huge mass of stellar gas and dust that contracts under the force of its own gravity to form one or more galaxies.

proton   A subatomic particle that carries a positive electromagnetic charge. A proton is one of the two particles that can form the nucleus of an atom; the other is the neutron.

prototype   A full-size working version of a machine or other object that is under development.

pylon   In airplane design, a strong post used for attaching engines, fuel tanks, weaponry, or other components to the wings or body of an airplane.

quanta   The plural of QUANTUM.

quantum   The smallest unit of matter or energy that can be identified or theorized.

quantum bit (qubit)   A subatomic particle that has been altered to serve as a data-processing unit in a quantum computer.

quantum computer   A computer in which subatomic particles, rather than electronic transistors, serve as the basic information storage and processing units.

quantum computing   A field of computer science that seeks to use the principles of quantum mechanics in the construction of extremely fast, powerful computers.

quantum jump (quantum leap)   The rapid transition of an atomic particle or energy unit from one energy state to another with no intermediate stage.

quantum mechanics   The branch of physics that seeks to explain how energy works and how atoms and subatomic particles behave.

quark   Subatomic particles that make up protons and neutrons, which contain three quarks each. The work *quark* was included as a nonsense syllable created by the author James Joyce for his book *Finnegans Wake*. The word was given its current meaning by Murray Gell-Mann, one of two physicists who first suggested the existence of these particles.

quark confinement The behavior exhibited if a quark starts to move away from the other two quarks present within a proton or a neutron. The other two quarks will pull on the wandering quark with a force strong enough to keep the proton or neutron together.

qubit *See* QUANTUM BIT.

ray-tracing A way to determine how objects in a virtual world would be illuminated by calculating the path light rays would take from the viewer's eye to the objects. In effect, this method involves pretending to make light waves "back up" from the eyes to the objects in a virtual environment.

real time The actual time in which a process or event takes place. In computing terms, real time means a computer or a network can respond to a user's input or actions quickly enough to seem instantaneous.

reality simulator A computer system specially designed to create and run virtual reality simulations.

refresh rate The number of times per second that a computer redraws the images it displays. For example, virtual reality systems need to maintain a refresh rate of 30 frames per second to create and maintain a sense of three-dimensional immersion.

rendering Creating a computer graphic image, in particular a three-dimensional image.

ribonucleic acid (RNA) A chemical within living cells that plays a central role in the formation of proteins.

router A specialized computer that directs information requests and data to their destination in a computer network.

scanning probe microscope A microscope that scans an extremely small object by passing a needle-like probe over its surface.

scientific method The process of explaining natural phenomena through observation, hypothesis, and experimentation. The scientific method also involves verification of one's work by other scientists, a process also known as "peer review."

second-generation computers Computers whose circuitry used transistors as switches, replacing vacuum tubes. Second-generation computers also used magnetic cores for memory and magnetic tape for data input, output, and storage. The second generation of computing technology covers the period from 1959 to 1964.

semiconductor A material that provides partial resistance to an electrical current flowing through itself; it is neither a good insulator nor a good conductor. Its properties can be altered with other chemicals so it can serve as an insulator or a conductor. Silicon, found in ordinary sand, is a semiconductor material.

semisynthetic A drug or other substance that comes from the chemical processing of natural materials.

serial processing The technique of using a single processing unit to work through a series of computations, one right after another.

server A computer that stores information for a network and distributes this information to other computers.

shell In physics, one of many regions around an atom's nucleus in which electrons orbit.

signature In physics, a set of frequencies or other characteristics that distinguishes a particular force from others.

six-degree-of-freedom (6DOF) Allowing a virtual reality user to move along and spin around all three axes of the three-dimensional world.

sonic tracker A position tracker that monitors movement using tiny microphones that pick up ultrasonic pulses from a fixed emitter.

sound waves Disturbances in the air or other materials that humans can interpret as sound.

squall line A string of thunderstorms that forms on the leading edge of a cold front.

stereoscopic vision The visual perception of length, width, and depth.

strain In biology, a subspecies of a bacteria or other microbe.

subatomic particles Tiny particles of matter such as electrons, protons, and neutrons that make up atoms.

supercluster A cluster formed by a gathering of galactic clusters.

supercomputer A very fast and very powerful computer that is able to perform a great number of mathematical operations in a very short time. Supercomputers usually are the fastest, and most expensive, computers available at any given time.

superconductor A material that can conduct electricity with little or no resistance.

supernova An exploding star that briefly outshines all the other stars in its galaxy.

teleoperation, telepresence, telerobotics Three terms for the technique of using virtual reality displays to operate remotely controlled robots or other machinery.

template A physical model, pattern, or gauge used to accurately make identical copies of a mechanical part or other object.

third-generation computers Computers whose components incorporated integrated circuits, which replaced circuit boards on which transistors, switches, and other devices were individually wired. These computers could process as many as 10 million instructions per second. Magnetic disks, both those of solid metal and those of flexible plastic covered by magnetic material, joined magnetic tape for storing data. The operating systems of these computers allowed for multiple, simultaneous use. The third generation of computing technology covers the period from 1964 to 1970.

three-degree-of-freedom (3DOF) Allowing a virtual reality user to move along the three axes of the three-dimensional world but not to spin around them.

three-dimensional mouse (3-D mouse) *See* MOUSE, 3-D.

thymine A chemical base present in DNA but not RNA.

transducer Any device or material that converts one form of energy to another. For example, a radio speaker, which takes electrical impulses and converts them to sound waves, is a form of transducer.

transistor An electronic component based around a semiconductor that can be used as a switch in an electric circuit. Transistors are smaller than vacuum tubes and generated far less heat. The development of transistors led to lighter, smaller computers.

tuple space A kind of shared memory in which the items in the memory have no computer address. In effect, this means that any task in tuple space can be accessed without regard to its location within memory or to the order of the items to be processed.

ultrasonic A sound wave with a higher frequency than that which humans can hear.

uracil A chemical base present in RNA but not DNA.

vacuum tube A closed glass tube from which all air has been removed and which contains one or more electric wires. Vacuum tubes were used as switches in many early computers.

vector processing A data processing technique in which a single operation, such as addition or multiplication, is carried out simultaneously on a list of numbers, speeding up the calculation of answers.

VET *See* VIRTUAL ENVIRONMENT TECHNOLOGY.

virtual Existing in theory or in the imagination but not in fact. Since the late 1970s, *virtual* also has come to mean just about anything that exists as a computer file or that can be accomplished using computer networks.

virtual environment A three-dimensional, immersive, interactive world designed for use in virtual reality.

virtual environment technology (VET)   Another term for virtual reality.

virtual presence   Another term for virtual reality.

virtual reality   A form of computer technology that creates the effect of immersing its user in a three-dimensional, computer-generated artificial world.

VR   *See* VIRTUAL REALITY.

wand   An effector that acts much like a 3-D mouse but is shaped like a television remote control or a joystick without a base.

wave   A pulse of energy that travels along or through something. There are two types of waves. Transverse waves, such as ocean waves, cause vibrations that are perpendicular to their path of movement. Longitudinal or compression waves, such as sound waves, cause vibrations that are parallel to their path of movement.

weaponized   Engineered into a form that is portable, easily distributed, and able to infect a wider population than it could in its original form.

wind shear   A short-distance change in the speed and direction of a wind. Wind shear in the form of the sudden, powerful microbursts that sometimes form over airports can cause aircraft to stall and crash.

wind tunnel   A structure equipped with a powerful fan that is used to test the aerodynamic properties, such as wind resistance and flight abilities, of airplanes, automobiles, buildings, and other objects.

wired glove   A glove-shaped effector that monitors the position of a user's hand and how far the user's fingers bend.

wireframe model   In computer animation, the skeleton of an image showing its basic structure and its general surface outline.

workstation   A very fast, very powerful personal computer designed specifically for advanced computer graphics or other projects that involve intensive calculations.

World Wide Web (WWW)   A subset of the Internet that presents information in a form that mimics pages from magazines or advertising brochures. Web pages can be connected via hyperlinks.

FURTHER READING

"A Doctorate in Chess, Supercomputing." Reuters news wire/CNET News.com, June 4, 2001. Available on-line. URL: http://news.cnet.com/news/0-1006-200-6185074.html.

"Artificial Intelligence: More Power for Games, Voice Recognition." Gannett On-line, April 3, 2002. Available on-line. URL: http://www.gannettonline.com/e/trends/15000575.html.

"Artificial Intelligence Returns—For Now." Forbes.com, June 25, 2001. Available on-line. URL: http://www.forbes.com/2001/06/25/0625dvorak.html.

"At Cornell, Cluster of Pentium Processors Becomes a Supercomputer." ScienceDaily Magazine, Thursday, October 7, 1999. Available on-line. URL: http://www.sciencedaily.com/releases/1999/10/991007083326.htm.

Augarten, Stan. *Bit by Bit: An Illustrated History of Computers.* New York: Ticknor & Fields, 1984.

Boyer, Carl B. *A History of Mathematics.* Revised by Uta C. Merzbach. New York: Wiley, 1991.

Brain, Marshall. "How Semiconductors Work." Available on-line. URL: www.howstuffworks.com/diode. Downloaded January 31, 2003.

Brand, Stewart. "Founding Father." *Wired,* March 2001, pp. 144–153.

Broersma, Matthew. "HP Creates Off-the-Shelf Supercomputer." CNET News.com, October 4, 2001. Available on-line. URL: http://news.cnet.com/news/0-1003-200-7409795.html.

Campbell-Kelly, Martin, and William Aspray. *Computer: A History of the Information Machine.* New York: Basic Books, 1996.

Carnoy, David. "Life in the Fast Lane: A Guide to the Internet's Best Broadband Destinations." *Fortune,* October 9, 2000, p. 308.

Ceruzzi, Paul E. *A History of Modern Computing.* Cambridge, Mass.: MIT Press, 1998.

Colvin, Geoffrey. "Confessions of a Transistor Hog." *Fortune,* June 25, 2001, p. 56

"Computing after Silicon." *Technology Review*, September/October 1999, pp. 92–96.

Crothers, Brooke. "Will Japan Beat U.S. in Supercomputers?" CNET News. com, June 14, 1999. Available on-line. URL: http://news.cnet.com/news/ 0-1003-200-343552.html.

DeTar, James. "Supercomputer Inventor Seymour Cray." *Investor's Business Daily*, February 2, 2001, page A3.

DiCarlo, Lisa. "Blade Servers Sharpen Data Revolution." Forbes.com, April 4, 2002. Available on-line. URL: http://www.forbes.com/2002/04/04/ 0404blades.html.

"Doctors Warn of Gaming's Health Risks." Reuters news wire/CNET News.com, February 1, 2002. Available on-line. URL: http://news.com. com/2100-1040-827666.html.

Fairley, Peter. "The Microphotonics Revolution." *Technology Review*, July/August 2000, pp. 38–44.

Foust, Jeff. "Calling All Idle Computers." *Technology Review*, September/October 1999, p. 104.

Freedman, David H. "The Great Quantum Number Cruncher." *Discover*, January 1999, pp. 90–96.

Gill, Lisa. "What Supercomputers Can and Cannot Do—Yet." NewsFactor, June 17, 2002. Available on-line. URL: http://www.NewsFactor.com.

———. "HP to Build Linux Supercomputer for U.S." NewsFactor, April 17, 2002. Available on-line. URL: http://www.NewsFactor.com.

"Grandaddy [sic] of Commercial PCs Hits 50." Associated Press, special to CNET News.com, June 15, 2001. Available on-line. URL: http://news. cnet.com/news/0-1003-200-6288274.html.

Hargrove, William H., Forrest M. Hoffman, and Thomas Sterling. "The Do-It-Yourself Supercomputer." *Scientific American*, August 2001, pp. 72–79.

Hesseldahl, Arik. "Happy Birthday, PC." Forbes.com, August 12, 2001. Available on-line. URL: http://www.forbes.com/2001/08/12/0812pcanniv. html.

Heudin, Jean-Claude, ed. *Virtual Worlds: Synthetic Universes, Digital Life, and Complexity*. Reading, Mass.: Perseus Books, 1999.

Hillner, Jennifer. "Fire Works." *Wired*, June 2000, pp. 94–95.

Hiltzik, Michael. "A.I. Reboots." *Technology Review*, March 2002, pp. 46–55.

Hummer, Caroline. "IBM to Link Government Computers in Powerful Grid." Reuters news wire/Yahoo! News, March 22, 2002. Available on-line. URL: http://story.news.yahoo.com.

"IBM Linux Supercomputers Land Oil Deal." Bloomberg News/CNET News.com, May 25, 2001. Available on-line. URL: http://news.cnet.com/ news/0-1003-200-6043774.html.

"IBM's Biotech Resurgence." Forbes.com, June 25, 2001. Available on-line. URL: http://www.forbes.com/2001/06/25/0625ibm.html.

"Japan Claims Fastest Computer Title." Reuters news wire/CNET News. com, April 21, 2002. Available on-line. URL: http://news.com.com/ 2102-1001-887717.html.

Jossi, Frank. "Quantum's Leap." *Wired*, December 2000, p. 112.

"Laying Down the Law." *Technology Review*, May 2001, pp. 64–68.

Leyden, Peter. "Moore's Law Repealed, Sort Of." *Wired*, May 1997, pp. 167–168.

Lemos, Robert. "Supercomputer Kings Stand Tall in New Rankings." CNET News.com, May 16, 2002. Available on-line. URL: http://news.com.com/ 2100-1001-916038.html.

Lohr, Steve. "IBM Opening a $2.5 Billion Specialized Chip Plant." *New York Times*, August 1, 2002. Available on-line. URL: http://www.nytimes.com/ 2002/08/01/business/01BLUE.html.

Markoff, John. "IBM Gets Contract for Weather Supercomputer." *New York Times*, June 1, 2002. Available on-line. URL: http://www.nytimes.com/ 2002/06/01/technology/01SUPE.html.

———. "Japanese Supercomputer Finds a Home in Alaska." *New York Times*, June 14, 2002. Available on-line. URL: http://www.nytimes.com/2002/06/ 14/technology/14SUPE.html.

———. "Japanese Computer Is World's Fastest, as U.S. Falls Back." *New York Times*, April 20, 2002. Available on-line. URL: http://www.nytimes.com/ 2002/04/20/technology/20COMP.html.

Martell, Duncan. "Intel Claims World's Smallest, Fastest Transistor." Reuters news wire/Yahoo! News, June 9, 2001. Available on-line. URL: http://dailynews.yahoo.com.

———. "National Science Foundation to Fund Supercomputer." Reuters news wire/Yahoo! News, August 9, 2001. Available on-line. URL: http://dailynews.yahoo.com.

McDonald, Tim. "The Shape of Computer Chips to Come." NewsFactor/Yahoo! News, May 1, 2002. Available on-line. URL: http://www.newsfactor.com.

Masson, Terrence. *CG 101: A Computer Graphics Industry Reference*. Indianapolis, Ind.: New Riders Publishing, 1999.

Monastersky, Richard. "Why Is the Pacific So Big? Look Down Deep." *Science News*, October 5, 1996, p. 213.

Morton, Oliver. "Gene Machine." *Wired*, July 2001, pp. 148–159.

Murray, Charles J. *The Supermen: The Story of Seymour Cray and the Technical Wizards behind the Supercomputer*. New York: Wiley, 1997.

"NCAR's 'Blue Sky' Supercomputer Technology to Spur Climate, Weather Research." ScienceDaily, November 20, 2001. Available on-line. URL: http://www.sciencedaily.com/releases/2001/11/011120050712.htm.

"NSF-Funded Terascale Computing System Ranks as World's Second Fastest; Pittsburgh-Based Computer Hits Peak of Six Trillion Operations per Second." Available on-line. URL: http://www.sciencedaily.com/releases/ 2001/11/011112075100.html.

Packer, Randall, and Ken Jordan, eds. *Multimedia: From Wagner to Virtual Reality*. New York: Norton, 2001.

Pascovitz, David. "Monsters in a Box." *Wired*, December 2000, pp. 340–347.

Peterson, Ivars. "Computation Takes a Quantum Leap." *Science News*, August 26, 1997, p. 132.

———. "Fine Lines for Chips." *Science News*, November 8, 1997, pp. 302–303.

———. "NSF Funds New Computing Partnerships." *Science News*, April 5, 1997, p. 204.

Pimentel, Ken, and Kevin Teixeira. *Virtual Reality: Through the New Looking Glass*. 2d ed. New York: McGraw-Hill, 1995.

"Planet Internet." *Technology Review*, March 2002, pp. 80–85.

Rheingold, Howard. "You Got The Power." *Wired*, August 2000, pp. 176–184.

———. *Virtual Reality*. New York: Simon & Schuster, 1991.

Riordan, Michael. "The Incredible Shrinking Transistor." *Technology Review*, November/December 1997, pp. 46–52.

Rothfeder, Jeffrey. *Minds over Matter: A New Look at Artificial Intelligence*. New York: Simon & Schuster, 1985.

Schwarz, Frederic D. "Happy Birthday, ENIAC." *Invention & Technology* 12, no. 1 (summer 1996): 6–7.

Segaller, Stephen. *Nerds 2.0.1: A Brief History of the Internet*. New York: TV Books, 1998.

Shankland, Stephen. "Buddy, Can You Spare Some Processing Time?" CNET News.com, September 1, 2000. Available on-line. URL: http://news.cnet.com/news/0-1003-202-2671550.html.

———. "IBM Exceeds Expectations with Supercomputer." CNET News.com, June 28, 2000. Available on-line. URL: http://news.cnet.com/news/0-1003-202-2167700.html.

———. "IBM Supercomputer Anniversary Overshadowed by Successor." CNET News.com, October 28, 1999. Available on-line. URL: http://news.cnet.com/news/0-1006-200-1424667.html.

———. "Linux Could Power New Supercomputer." CNET News.com, October 29, 1999. Available on-line. URL: http://news.cnet.com/news/0-1003-200-1425245.html.

———. "Supercomputers Getting Super-duper." CNET News.com, June 20, 2002. Available on-line. URL: http://news.com.com/2100-1001-938032.html.

Sterling, Thomas. "How to Build a Hypercomputer." *Scientific American*, July 2001, pp. 38–45.

Vorwald, Alan, and Frank Clark. *Computers! From Sand Table to Electronic Brain*. New York: McGraw-Hill, 1964.

Voss, David. "Chips Go Nano." *Technology Review*, March/April 1999, pp. 55–57.

———. "The Virtual Alchemists." *Technology Review*, July/August 1999, pp. 56–61.

Waldrop, M. Mitchell. "Computing's Johnny Appleseed." *Technology Review*, January/February 2000, p. 66.

Waldrop, M. Mitchell. "Grid Computing." *Technology Review*, May 2002, pp. 31–37.

———. "No, This Man Invented the Internet." *Forbes ASAP.* Available online. URL: http://www.forbes.com/asap/2000/1127/105.html.

Wen, Howard. "Sim Dizzy: Does Half-Life Make You Sick? Well, You're Not Alone. Plenty of Gamers Suffer from Simulation Sickness." *Salon*, August 11, 2000. Available on-line. URL: http://www.salon.com.

Yaukey, John. "Breakthroughs." Gannett On-line, April 3, 2002. Available online. URL: http://www.gannettonline.com/e/trends/15000570.html.

WORLD WIDE
WEB SITES

The following list is a sample of sites on the World Wide Web that provide up-to-date information on supercomputers and their uses. The list includes some of the top supercomputer manufacturers, academic and governmental research centers, and independent computing organizations in the world. The addresses for the sites were current as of January 2003; owing to the nature of the Internet and the rapid changes that can take place there, however, they may have changed after this book was published. If so, and if the site has not gone out of business, the new addresses might be found by searching the Web for the site's name. Otherwise, running a search for the terms such as "supercomputers," "supercomputing applications," or "scientific computing" should yield enough information to satisfy anyone's curiosity.

Academic and Governmental Sites

1. National Center for Supercomputing Applications, at the University of Illinois at Urbana-Champaign: http://www.ncsa.uiuc.edu
2. San Diego Supercomputer Center, at the University of California, San Diego: http://www.sdsc.edu
3. National Science Foundation: http://www.nsf.gov
4. Arctic Region Supercomputing Center, at the University of Alaska, Fairbanks: http://www.arsc.edu
5. Pittsburgh Supercomputing Center, at Carnegie Mellon University in Pittsburgh, Pennsylvania: http://www.psc.edu

6. Ohio Supercomputing Center, at Ohio State University in Columbus, Ohio: http:/www.osc.edu

Computer Organizations

1. Association for Computing Machinery, a professional organization for computer researchers and industry professionals: http://www.acm.org
2. IEEE Computer Society, a professional organization for computer researchers organized under the Institute of Electric and Electronic Engineers: http://www.computer.org
3. Top500.org, the Web site for a twice-yearly ranking of the most powerful supercomputers in the world. The site also contains general information on supercomputers: http://www.top500.org

Computer History Organizations

1. Computer History Museum: http://www.computerhistory.org
2. The Charles Babbage Institute at the University of Minnesota's Center for the History of Information Technology: http://www.cbi.umn.edu
3. "John W. Mauchley and the Development of the ENIAC Computer," exhibition at the University of Pennsylvania: http://www.library.upenn.edu/special/gallery/mauchly/jwmintro.html
4. Official Bletchley Park historical Web site: http://www.bletchleypark.org.uk

Supercomputer Manufacturers

1. Cray Research, one of the companies founded by supercomputing pioneer Seymour Cray: http://www.cray.com
2. Hewlett-Packard, one of the oldest electronics firms in the United States and one of the nation's top supercomputer manufacturers; early in the 21st century, it purchased another computer manufacturer, Compaq, which also had a strong presence in the supercomputer market: http://www.hp.com
3. Hitachi, Ltd., a Japanese electronics firm that makes some of the world's fastest supercomputers: http://www.hitachi.com
4. NEC Corporation, another prominent Japanese supercomputer manufacturer: http://www.nec.com
5. SGI (Silicon Graphics, Inc.), a company that manufactures high-speed computers and workstations for graphics and other applications: http://www.sgi.com

Other Sites

1. Intel's Philanthropic Peer-to-Peer Program, one of the many distributed computing efforts that uses computers linked over the Internet to analyze data. Included among the research projects that Intel has supported are programs that used screensaver time to find possible cures for anthrax: http://www.intel.com/cure.
2. The Earth Simulator Center, the home of the top-rated supercomputer in 2002: http://www.es.jamstec.go.jp/esc/eng/index.html.
3. Beowulf.org, a Web site that features information about Beowulf cluster supercomputers. The site is operated by a Beowulf cluster manufacturer, Scyld Computing Corporation: http://www.beowulf.org.
4. Stories of The Development of Large Scale Scientific Computing at Lawrence Livermore National Laboratory. The computer history site is assembled by former researchers at the laboratory: http://www.computer-history.info.

INDEX

Italic page numbers indicate illustrations.